Inventions of Farewell:

A Book of Elegies

Inventions of Farewell:
A Book of Elegies

Edited and with an introduction by

Sandra M. Gilbert

W. W. Norton & Company
New York • London

The text of this book is composed in Electra with the display set in Electra Bold
Composition by Allentown Digital Services Division of R.R. Donnelley & Sons
Company
Manufacturing by Haddon Craftsmen
Book design by JAM Design

Library of Congress Cataloging-in-Publication Data

Inventions of farewell : a book of elegies / edited with an introduction
by Sandra M. Gilbert.
p.   cm.
Includes index.
ISBN 0-393-04972-8
1. Elegiac poetry, English. 2. Elegiac poetry, American. I. Gilbert, Sandra M.

PR1195.E5 I58 2001
821.008'03548—dc21   00-048954

W. W. Norton & Company, Inc., 500 Fifth Avenue, New York, N.Y. 10110
www.wwnorton.com

W. W. Norton & Company Ltd., 10 Coptic Street, London WC1A 1PU

1 2 3 4 5 6 7 8 9 0

Table of Contents

Acknowledgments

Although my deep immersion in the poems of mourning that I collect in this anthology really began with grief at the death of my husband, Elliot Gilbert, in 1991, the work on the book itself that I've conducted over the last two years has been facilitated by the love and friendship of the living, and by many gestures of practical support as well. I want in particular to thank the Soros Foundation's Project on Death in America, the National Endowment for the Humanities, the University of California President's Office, and the University of California, Davis, for generous grants in aid of my research, and I am also grateful to the Bogliasco Foundation for a stimulating month-long residency at the beautiful Liguria Study Center, where I was able to complete much of my writing.

Among individuals who've helped me, I offer special thanks to my agent, Ellen Levine; my editor, Jill Bialosky (and her assistant, Drake Bennett); my former research assistant, Christopher Sindt; and a host of other wonderful graduate students at U.C. Davis, whose lively comments on the elegy, on modernist visions of the afterlife, and on the poetry of mourning in general have contributed in countless vital ways to my thinking on this subject. That thinking has also been influenced by advice from a number of other wise counselors for whose aid I'm grateful, most notably my friends Joanne Feit Diehl, Marilyn Hacker, and Carolyn Kizer, all of whom helped me think about the shape and substance of my table of contents, as did my son, Roger Gilbert, and my daughter Susanna Gilbert. In addition, I'm much indebted to my ever-resourceful research assistant, Hayward Augustus Rose, whose patience, persistence, and commitment even to the smallest details of this project helped bring the book into being. And finally, for ongoing moral support and emotional nurturance, I must thank not just my literary offspring Roger and Susanna but my always practical daughter Kathy, along with my true and trusty living-and-traveling companion, David Gale.

"Omissions," as Marianne Moore famously observed, "are not accidents," and though she was referring to her visions and revisions of her own work, her comment is singularly apropos to the anthologist who must battle for permissions in an era when all too many publishers are inclined, at least initially, to ask fees that editors of low-budget collections simply can't afford. In fact, because one or two publishers and/or agents demanded truly exorbitant permissions fees, there are a few important twentieth-century elegies, still in copyright, that I have had reluctantly to omit from this book. My pain at these omissions, however, has been more than assuaged by the courtesy of the many, many poets and editors whose generosity and flexibility have helped me assemble what I hope will be a powerful documentation of the ways in which some of the finest writers in the English language have confronted loss and grief over the centuries, from the late Middle Ages to the end of the 1990s. Indeed, it is for the generosity as well as the genius of the poets, in particular, that I reserve my profoundest gratitude.

Introduction

"I have heard it said that crows have funerals, or something akin to funerals, for other crows," mused the late *Newsweek* columnist Meg Greenfield in 1996. Meditating on the fate of what might be called ceremonial mourning—the kind of mourning expressed not just in tears and wails of lamentation but through religion's traditional funeral rituals and the time-honored literary forms of elegy and eulogy—she was wondering how a skeptical, hedonistic, often death-denying culture can find appropriate public and private ways of articulating grief.[1] When faced, today, with the death of someone we cherish, how do we show, and say, we're sorry?

Historically, both priests and poets have helped us find a language for loss, often a highly stylized and dramatic vocabulary through which to shape the otherwise inexpressible grief of bereavement. The need for such rituals is deep rooted in just about every society; indeed, if Greenfield's surmise that even "crows have funerals" is accurate, such a need may transcend our own species.[2] Yet like a number of sociologists and historians, the *Newsweek* columnist couldn't help noticing that we live in an age marked by considerable confusion about what might be called "procedures" for grieving.

That at this turn of the century mourning has become not so much electric as *eclectic* was made quite clear in early September 1997, when what Walt Whitman called "the tolling tolling bells' perpetual clang" was

1. Greenfield, "Respecting the Dead," *Newsweek*, April 22, 1996.

2. For instance, in her *Fragments on the Deathwatch* (Boston: Beacon Press, 1998), Louise Harmon meditates on "elephant grief," noting that elephants "attend the births and deaths of members of their species" and describing the mourning behavior of one herd after "the death of an old bull." Citing a *National Geographic* article, she describes how the surviving elephants "approached his body in twos and threes, 'sweeping their trunks slowly over him, not touching him for the most part but maintaining an inch of distance between his skin and the moist tips of their trunks. The ritual was more impressive for its silence.' " (Cf. Dereck Joubert, "Eyewitness to an Elephant Wake," *National Geographic*, May 1991: 39, 40.)

heard worldwide, as the funeral cortège of Diana, Princess of Wales, passed solemnly through the flower-banked streets of London. A few weeks later, scornfully describing "the kitsch of the Diana shrines," the *New Yorker* reporter Adam Gopnik exclaimed in an essay entitled "Crazy Piety" that "for two weeks good gray London took on the look of Lourdes or Fatima, with vast heaps of floral bouquets and honey-colored Teddy bears and hand-scrawled messages that seemed less like funeral tributes than like the contents of some vast piñata, filled with party favors, that someone had broken above" the city. And indeed, as most of the millions who watched the televised rites will also recall, the princess's funeral ceremony itself was marked by a similarly odd concatenation of the traditional and the trivial, craziness and piety, sentimentality and solemnity. Anglican ritual and Elton John, the grave words of the King James Bible and the souped-up warble of the American Bible Belt echoed through Westminster Abbey like radio frequencies colliding in the stratosphere. If Diana herself was half a jet-setting single mom and half a populist madonna, her death—taken as a representative symbolic as well as literal experience of loss—illuminated the ambiguities of modern mourning.

"Brightness falls from the air; / Queens have died young and fair," lamented Thomas Nashe in the 1590s, and "Goodbye England's rose. . . . This torch we'll always carry / For our nation's golden child," crooned Elton John, recycling not Nashe's poem but his own earlier tribute to another queen who died young and fair—Marilyn Monroe—as he produced what was to be one of the greatest hits of the decade, if not the century. Well, harumphed Gopnik, in the excesses of the princess's funeral, which was "in many ways a triumph of the popular, intuitive version of the Old Religion [i.e., Roman Catholicism], it was possible to discern a glimmer of religious feeling, of a very traditional kind."[3] Just a "glimmer," though, for in this era where the guidelines of tradition are increasingly blurry, public mourning is usually more notable for its minimalism than for its excess. In fact, a few words spoken at the austere funeral of Ophelia in act 5 of *Hamlet* summarize questions that haunt all too many modern mourners. "What ceremony else?" the dead girl's grieving brother, Laertes, poignantly asks the officiating priest, wondering

3. Gopnik, "Crazy Piety," *The New Yorker*, Sept. 29, 1997, 36.

"Must there no more be done?" *What ceremonies else* do we have, nowadays, for those who are bereaved? What more must be—*can* be—done to assuage grief?

This anthology is designed to offer some answers to such questions by introducing readers to at least one way of mourning that has persisted through massive cultural and theological turmoil, even while it has also, of course, been transformed by the fluctuations of history: the form of lyric poetry known as the elegy. For centuries, after all, poets have lamented the mortal losses that all of us must inexorably encounter. Whether (with Dylan Thomas) counseling readers to "Rage, rage against the dying of the light" or (with Walt Whitman) taking comfort in the serene arrival, "sooner or later," of "delicate death," most writers of verse have "sooner or later" had to face bereavement. Aesthetic assumptions and poetic styles have altered over the centuries, yet the great and often terrifying themes of time, change, age, and death are timeless, even though cultural imaginings of them may differ radically. As we begin a new millennium, therefore, having just in a sense "put to rest" the last two thousand years of our communal past, it seems particularly appropriate to turn our attention to literary encounters with life's end as well as to the ways in which such encounters have been inflected by the public history and personal stories they both record and mourn.

Taken together, the traditional and not-so-traditional elegies included in this anthology dramatize the range of strategies through which poets have long sought to confront and confound mortality. Representing both what endures and what varies in modes of lamentation, *Inventions of Farewell* collects English-language poems of mourning from the late Middle Ages to the present, focusing especially on works by modern and contemporary writers but also including such classics as Milton's "Lycidas," Shelley's "Adonais," and Whitman's "When Lilacs Last in the Dooryard Bloom'd."

What endures: This book is organized thematically in order to emphasize common questions, concerns, and tactics with which poets have for generations approached and lamented loss. As the table of contents indicates, there are two main sections: an opening section tracing the visions of death and dying—the necessities of mortality, as it were—that implicitly or explicitly shape a number of elegies; and a longer, second section cataloging the kinds of losses that poets have traditionally sought to record and sometimes even redress. Part I is then subdivided into four groups: poems recounting death scenes, poems focusing on "viewings" of the body in death, poems enacting funeral rituals or other ceremonies of separation, and poems imagining (in a whole range of ways) the ultimate fate of those who have died—perhaps a traditional "afterlife" or perhaps something very different. Similarly, after beginning with poems ostensibly mourning mythic figures in the pastoral tradition of which "Lycidas" and "Adonais" are the most famous English-language examples, Part II includes subsections devoted to poems lamenting a spectrum of different losses—the deaths of parents, of spouses and lovers, of children, of friends, of other poets, of the great and famous, and of the victims of war and other violence, along with what the critic Jahan Ramazani has called "self-elegies" and more generalized meditations on mortality.

What varies: Within individual sections, I have arranged poems chronologically in order to show how historical and cultural differences have produced aesthetic changes. In particular, my organization of texts is meant to illuminate the often strikingly transformed procedures for mourning devised by so many poets in our own era of mounting theological and social confusion. Thus *Inventions of Farewell*, my title for the anthology, is drawn from Wallace Stevens's "The Owl in the Sarcophagus," the poet's beautiful, mysterious, and curiously mystical elegy for his friend Henry Church. In this work, contemplating what he called the "mythology of modern death" that is the product of a skeptical age, the author of that post-Christian masterpiece "Sunday Morning" outlined a poetics of grief in which consolation comes from "inventions of farewell." Such "forms of thought" may be merely "monsters of elegy," Stevens concedes—mutations of a genre infected by what Matthew Arnold long ago called the "strange disease of modern life"—but they are also the "children of a desire that is the will, / Even of death," a will to art and speech.

The new millennium has dawned with a curious combination of excitement and confusion. On the one hand, this twenty-first century that had long seemed so dreamlike, so impossibly apocalyptic, has plunged us into a world of virtual fantasy and fantastic virtuosity. We send rockets to

Mars and e-mail to cyberspace, replace worn-out organs and speculate on genetic engineering. In such a high-tech context, it may be hard for some people to focus on human vulnerability—the mortality of the flesh. Perhaps for this reason, death itself is often considered a kind of "unspeakable" event. As I began my research into the history of the elegy, I encountered a remarkable anecdote by a fellow investigator of what Stevens called "modern death": "When I called the American Cancer Society to request permission to include some of their materials in [my] book, their representative responded: 'Absolutely not. In no way do we want to be associated with a book on death. We want to emphasize the positive aspects of cancer only.' "[4]

What, though, are the implications of such an attitude toward dying, death, and the dead not only for those who are dying but for those who must mourn them? More specifically, with what "monsters of elegy" have recent poets responded to the anxious circumlocutions that mark this "mythology of modern death"? From the mid-twentieth-century elegies produced by (among others) Robert Lowell, Allen Ginsberg, Elizabeth Bishop, and Sylvia Plath to the recent writings of poets including Ruth Stone, Thom Gunn, Donald Hall, Sharon Olds, Tess Gallagher, and Paul Monette, the poems in *Inventions of Farewell* arguably trace the evolution of a defiant contemporary poetics of grief that has been shaped by factors ranging from what the American critic J. Hillis Miller once called the "disappearance of God" to the twentieth-century privatization and medicalization of death along with the "rejection" of mourning that have been most notably studied by the French historian Philippe Ariès.

Ariès's work is of particular interest here. Examining "western attitudes toward death" from the medieval "tame death" to the contemporary medicalized death, Ariès has incisively demonstrated that the necessities of dying and mourning have never before been seen as so *scandalous:* on the one hand, we live in an age when most people die in hospitals or hospices, and this medicalization of death has "eliminated [death's] character of public ceremony, and made it a private act," and on the other hand, associated with such privatization has been the "sec-

4. Quoted in David Wendell Moller, *Confronting Death: Values, Institutions, and Human Mortality* (New York: Oxford University Press, 1996), p. vii.

ond great milestone in the contemporary history of death"—the repudiation of most traditional modes of mourning. Yes, we do mourn but we don't usually "go into black," as, say, the Victorians did, and "bereavement counselors," hurrying us through the "stages of grief," briskly advise us to "get on with life" as quickly and efficiently as possible rather than "fixating" lingeringly on loss.

But as a number of social commentators have shown, the widespread modern rejection of long-standing, customary procedures for grieving, together with intellectual anxiety about the so-called disappearance of God, has for decades elicited not just high-cultural gloom but also popular confusion and distress. From Jessica Mitford's midcentury bestseller *The American Way of Death* (which vigorously critiqued "the malarkey that surrounds the usual kind of funeral") to the often bizarre outpourings of ceremonial improvisation that characterized Princess Diana's 1997 funeral, from the death counseling prescribed in the seventies by Elisabeth Kubler-Ross to the cheerful spiritualism propounded by James Van Praagh's recent bestseller *Talking to Heaven*, the social bewilderment fostered by changing mythologies of death has issued in a number of sometimes contradictory modes of encountering loss.

Adding special poignancy to unfilled needs for ceremonial grief are technological innovations that have transformed our relationship to history and memory—namely, the development of films and videos that allow us to see and hear the dead as if they were among the living. While such ghostly presences are unprecedented, they are especially unnerving in a cultural context where death is a scandal to be denied and grief an embarrassment to be deplored. Can the dead be in and of history and memory if we can still see them and hear them? Equally to the point, how can we bear witness to the absolute fact that they are *not* here?

Theological uncertainty coupled with technological virtuosity, the fate of the souls of the dead uncertain yet the bodies of the dead apparently alive on screen, grief as illness and illness as culpable: Taken together these phenomena might have stifled poetic "inventions of farewell." Yet contemporary poets resist the repression of death as resolutely as their great modernist precursors resisted the repression of sex. That we live in an era of calamitous worldwide human violence—of national as well as international murderousness—gives their work great urgency. Indeed, as a number of the elegies collected in this anthology reveal, even before the AIDS pandemic forced death and dying out of the closet, testimonial imperatives fostered by traumas like the Great War and the Holocaust evolved into *literary* modes of resistance to both regressive sentimentalizings of grief and cultural valedictions forbidding mourning.

Brooding on what Wallace Stevens once called the "handbook of heartbreak"—the compendium of losses one necessarily encounters in even the sunniest life—modern and postmodern poets have even in the midst of (or in defiance of) deepest sorrow composed countless stirring "inventions of farewell," a number of them represented in this volume. That all can draw on a powerful and empowering tradition of English-language elegies also represented here, a tradition reaching back some seven centuries to the time of Geoffrey Chaucer's talented contemporary William Dunbar and continuing on through the epochs of such dazzling figures as Shakespeare, Milton, Shelley, Tennyson, Dickinson, and Hardy, helps explain the strength of the work they produce. Yet as Stevens would no doubt have sought to remind us, this tradition that fortifies our contemporaries, like the "mythology of modern death" devised and revised by its inheritors, itself attests to the intensity of the desire that is the will to art.

I

Watching:

Visions of the Dying

and the Dead

1.

"Do Not Go Gentle":

Watching the Dying

"Do not go gentle into that good night. / Rage, rage against the dying of the light." The famous injunction is Dylan Thomas's, but as many of the poems in this section show, most of the dying *do* go gentle—or sedated—or anyway barely conscious into death's mysterious "good night." Yes, some lie down "sick at heart," like Lord Randall in the ancient ballad, while others pass "overhead" whimpering like the soul of Kipling's Danny Deever. But often what Emily Dickinson rightly calls the "Crisis" of mortality is nearly silent. With the speaker of Thomas Hood's "The Death-Bed," those who watch the dying must admit that life and death sometimes seem to dissolve into each other at the end, so that "We thought her dying when she slept. / And sleeping when she died!"

Yet the need to bear witness at this crucial time is deep and strong. As the poems here by Donald Hall, Douglas Dunn, Paul Monette, and Mark Doty testify, couples frequently cling to each other in a shadowy borderland, a place of liminal stillness in which what Thom Gunn defines as the "difficult enterprise" of dying must take place. And now and then in that transitional space of the death watch, those who attend (to) the dying are astonished, as Sharon Olds is, by a "lifting" of old prohibitions that exposes the body in its vulnerable nakedness and the soul in the purity of its desire for *being*.

ANON.

Lord Randall

"Oh where ha'e ye been, Lord Randall my son?
O where ha'e ye been, my handsome young man?"
    "I ha'e been to the wild wood: mother, make my bed soon,
    For I'm weary wi' hunting, and fain wald lie down."

"Where gat ye your dinner, Lord Randall my son?
Where gat ye your dinner, my handsome young man?"
    "I dined wi' my true love: mother, make my bed soon,
    For I'm weary wi' hunting, and fain wald lie down."

"What gat ye to your dinner, Lord Randall my son?
What gat ye to your dinner, my handsome young man?"
    "I gat eels boiled in broo: mother, make my bed soon,
    For I'm weary wi' hunting and fain wald lie down."

"What became of your bloodhounds, Lord Randall my son?
What became of your bloodhounds, my handsome young man?"
    "O they swelled and they died: mother, make my bed soon,
    For I'm weary wi' hunting and fain wald lie down."

"O I fear ye are poisoned, Lord Randall my son!
O I fear ye are poisoned, my handsome young man!"
    "Oh yes, I am poisoned: mother, make my bed soon,
    For I'm sick at the heart, and I fain wald lie down."

THOMAS HOOD

The Death-Bed

We watch'd her breathing thro' the night,
Her breathing soft and low,
As in her breast the wave of life
Kept heaving to and fro!

So silently we seemed to speak—
So slowly moved about!
As we had lent her half our powers
To eke her living out!

Our very hopes belied our fears
Our fears our hopes belied—
We thought her dying when she slept,
And sleeping when she died!

For when the morn came dim and sad—
And chill with early showers,
Her quiet eyelids closed—she had
Another morn than ours!

EMILY DICKINSON

'Twas Crisis—All the length had passed—(#1093)

'Twas Crisis—All the length had passed—
That dull—benumbing time
There is in Fever or Event—
And now the Chance had come—

The instant holding in it's claw
The privilege to live
Or warrant to report the Soul
The other side the Grave.

The Muscles grappled as with leads
That would not let the Will—
The Spirit shook the Adamant—
But could not make it feel.

The Second poised—debated—shot—
Another had begun—
And simultaneously, a Soul
Escaped the House unseen—

RUDYARD KIPLING

Danny Deever

"What are the bugles blowin' for?" said Files-on-Parade.
"To turn you out, to turn you out," the Colour-Sergeant said.
"What makes you look so white, so white?" said Files-on-Parade.
"I'm dreadin' what I've got to watch," the Colour-Sergeant said.
    For they're hangin' Danny Deever, you can hear the Dead March
        play,
    The regiment's in 'ollow square—they're hangin' him to-day;
    They've taken of his buttons off an' cut his stripes away,
    An' they're hangin' Danny Deever in the mornin'.

"What makes the rear-rank breathe so 'ard?" said Files-on-Parade.
"It's bitter cold, it's bitter cold," the Colour-Sergeant said.
"What makes that front-rank man fall down?" said Files-on-Parade.
"A touch o' sun, a touch o' sun," the Colour-Sergeant said.
    They are hangin' Danny Deever, they are marchin' of 'im round,
    They 'ave 'alted Danny Deever by 'is coffin on the ground;
    An' 'e'll swing in 'arf a minute for a sneakin' shootin' hound—
    O they're hangin' Danny Deever in the mornin'!

" 'Is cot was right-'and cot to mine," said Files-on-Parade.
" 'E's sleepin' out an' far to-night," the Colour-Sergeant said.
"I've drunk 'is beer a score o' times," said Files-on-Parade.
" 'E's drinkin' bitter beer alone," the Colour-Sergeant said.
    They are hangin' Danny Deever, you must mark 'im to 'is place,
    For 'e shot a comrade sleepin'—you must look 'im in the face;
    Nine 'undred of 'is county an' the Regiment's disgrace,
    While they're hangin' Danny Deever in the mornin'.

"What's that so black agin the sun?" said Files-on-Parade.
"It's Danny fightin' 'ard for life," the Colour-Sergeant said.
"What's that that whimpers over'ead?" said Files-on-Parade.

"It's Danny's soul that's passin' now," the Colour-Sergeant said.
  For they're done with Danny Deever, you can 'ear the quickstep play,
  The regiment's in column, an' they're marchin' us away;
  Ho! the young recruits are shakin', an' they'll want their beer to-day,
  After hangin' Danny Deever in the mornin'!

ROBERT FROST

"Out, Out—"

The buzz saw snarled and rattled in the yard
And made dust and dropped stove-length sticks of wood,
Sweet-scented stuff when the breeze drew across it.
And from there those that lifted eyes could count
Five mountain ranges one behind the other
Under the sunset far into Vermont.
And the saw snarled and rattled, snarled and rattled,
As it ran light, or had to bear a load.
And nothing happened: day was all but done.
Call it a day, I wish they might have said
To please the boy by giving him the half hour
That a boy counts so much when saved from work.
His sister stood beside them in her apron
To tell the "Supper." At the word, the saw,
As if to prove saws knew what supper meant,
Leaped out at the boy's hand, or seemed to leap—
He must have given the hand. However it was,
Neither refused the meeting. But the hand!
The boy's first outcry was a rueful laugh,
As he swung toward them holding up the hand,
Half in appeal, but half as if to keep
The life from spilling. Then the boy saw all—
Since he was old enough to know, big boy
Doing a man's work, though a child at heart—
He saw all spoiled. "Don't let him cut my hand off—
The doctor, when he comes. Don't let him, sister!"
So. But the hand was gone already.
The doctor put him in the dark of ether.
He lay and puffed his lips out with his breath.
And then—the watcher at his pulse took fright.

No one believed. They listened at his heart.
Little—less—nothing!—and that ended it.
No more to build on there. And they, since they
Were not the one dead, turned to their affairs.

WILLIAM CARLOS WILLIAMS

The Last Words of My English Grandmother

There were some dirty plates
and a glass of milk
beside her on a small table
near the rank, disheveled bed—

Wrinkled and nearly blind
she lay and snored
rousing with anger in her tones
to cry for food,

Gimme something to eat—
They're starving me—
I'm all right I won't go
to the hospital. No, no, no

Give me something to eat
Let me take you
to the hospital, I said
and after you are well

you can do as you please.
She smiled, Yes
you do what you please first
then I can do what I please—

Oh, oh, oh! she cried
as the ambulance men lifted
her to the stretcher—
Is this what you call

making me comfortable?
By now her mind was clear—
Oh you think you're smart
you young people,

she said, but I'll tell you
you don't know anything.
Then we started.
On the way

we passed a long row
of elms. She looked at them
awhile out of
the ambulance window and said,

What are all those
fuzzy-looking things out there?
Trees? Well, I'm tired
of them and rolled her head away.

D. H. LAWRENCE

Sorrow

Why does the thin grey strand
Floating up from the forgotten
Cigarette between my fingers,
Why does it trouble me?

Ah, you will understand;
When I carried my mother downstairs,
A few times only, at the beginning
Of her soft-foot malady,

I should find, for a reprimand
To my gaiety, a few long grey hairs
On the breast of my coat; and one by one
I watched them float up the dark chimney.

WILFRED OWEN

Dulce Et Decorum Est[1]

Bent double, like old beggars under sacks,
Knock-kneed, coughing like hags, we cursed through sludge,
Till on the haunting flares we turned our backs
And towards our distant rest began to trudge.
Men marched asleep. Many had lost their boots
But limped on, blood-shod. All went lame; all blind;
Drunk with fatigue; deaf even to the hoots
Of tired, outstripped Five-Nines that dropped behind.

Gas! GAS! Quick, boys!—An ecstasy of fumbling,
Fitting the clumsy helmets just in time;
But someone still was yelling out and stumbling,
And flound'ring like a man in fire or lime . . .
Dim, through the misty panes and thick green light,
As under a green sea, I saw him drowning.

In all my dreams, before my helpless sight,
He plunges at me, guttering, choking, drowning.

If in some smothering dreams you too could pace
Behind the wagon that we flung him in,
And watch the white eyes writhing in his face,
His hanging face, like a devil's sick of sin;
If you could hear, at every jolt, the blood
Come gargling from the froth-corrupted lungs,
Obscene as cancer, bitter as the cud
Of vile, incurable sores on innocent tongues,—
My friend, you would not tell with such high zest
To children ardent for some desperate glory,
The old Lie: Dulce et decorum est
Pro patria mori.

[1]From the Latin of Horace: "It is sweet and proper to die for one's country."

DYLAN THOMAS

Do Not Go Gentle into That Good Night

Do not go gentle into that good night,
Old age should burn and rave at close of day;
Rage, rage against the dying of the light.

Though wise men at their end know dark is right,
Because their words had forked no lightning they
Do not go gentle into that good night.

Good men, the last wave by, crying how bright
Their frail deeds might have danced in a green bay,
Rage, rage against the dying of the light.

Wild men who caught and sang the sun in flight,
And learn, too late, they grieved it on its way,
Do not go gentle into that good night.

Grave men, near death, who see with blinding sight
Blind eyes could blaze like meteors and be gay,
Rage, rage against the dying of the light.

And you, my father, there on the sad height,
Curse, bless, me now with your fierce tears, I pray.
Do not go gentle into that good night.
Rage, rage against the dying of the light.

DONALD HALL

Last Days

"It was reasonable
to expect." So he wrote. The next day,
      in a consultation room,
Jane's hematologist Letha Mills sat down,
      stiff, her assistant
standing with her back to the door.
      "I have terrible news,"
Letha told them. "The leukemia is back.
There's nothing to do."
The four of them wept. He asked how long,
      why did it happen now?
Jane asked only: "Can I die at home?"

        .   .   .

      Home that afternoon,
they threw her medicines into the trash.
      Jane vomited. He wailed
while she remained dry-eyed—silent,
      trying to let go. At night
he picked up the telephone to make
      calls that brought
a child or a friend into the horror.

        .   .   .

      The next morning,
they worked choosing among her poems
      for *Otherwise*, picked
hymns for her funeral, and supplied each
      other words as they wrote

and revised her obituary. The day after,
    with more work to do
on her book, he saw how weak she felt,
    and said maybe not now; maybe
later. Jane shook her head: "Now," she said.
    "We have to finish it now."
Later, as she slid exhausted into sleep,
    she said, "Wasn't that fun?
To work together? Wasn't that fun?"

                .   .   .

    He asked her, "What clothes
should we dress you in, when we bury you?"
    "I hadn't thought," she said.
"I wondered about the white salwar
    kameez," he said—
her favorite Indian silk they bought
    in Pondicherry a year
and a half before, which she wore for best
    or prettiest afterward.
She smiled. "Yes. Excellent," she said.
    He didn't tell her
that a year earlier, dreaming awake,
    he had seen her
in the coffin in her white salwar kameez.

                .   .   .

    Still, he couldn't stop
planning. That night he broke out with,
    "When Gus dies I'll
have him cremated and scatter his ashes
    on your grave!" She laughed
and her big eyes quickened and she nodded:
    "It will be good

for the daffodils." She lay pallid back
        on the flowered pillow:
"Perkins, how do you *think* of these things?"

                    .   .   .

        They talked about their
adventures—driving through England
        when they first married,
and excursions to China and India.
        Also they remembered
ordinary days—pond summers, working
        on poems together,
walking the dog, reading Chekhov
        aloud. When he praised
thousands of afternoon assignations
        that carried them into
bliss and repose on this painted bed,
        Jane burst into tears
and cried, "No more fucking. No more fucking!"

                    .   .   .

        Incontinent three nights
before she died, Jane needed lifting
        onto the commode.
He wiped her and helped her back into bed.
        At five he fed the dog
and returned to find her across the room,
        sitting in a straight chair.
When she couldn't stand, how could she walk?
        He feared she would fall
and called for an ambulance to the hospital,
        but when he told Jane,
her mouth twisted down and tears started.

"Do we have to?" He canceled.
Jane said, "Perkins, be with me when I die."

.   .   .

"Dying is simple," she said.
"What's worst is . . . *the separation.*"
    When she no longer spoke,
they lay alone together, touching,
        and she fixed on him
her beautiful enormous round brown eyes,
        shining, unblinking,
and passionate with love and dread.

.   .   .

One by one they came,
the oldest and dearest, to say goodbye
        to this friend of the heart.
At first she said their names, wept, and touched;
        then she smiled; then
turned one mouth-corner up. On the last day
        she stared silent goodbyes
with her hands curled and her eyes stuck open.

.   .   .

Leaving his place beside her,
where her eyes stared, he told her,
        "I'll put these letters
in the box." She had not spoken
        for three hours, and now Jane said
her last words: "O.K."
                            At eight that night,
        her eyes open as they stayed

until she died, brain-stem breathing
     started, he bent to kiss
her pale cool lips again, and felt them
     one last time gather
and purse and peck to kiss him back.

·   ·   ·

     In the last hours, she kept
her forearms raised with pale fingers clenched
     at cheek level, like
the goddess figurine over the bathroom sink.
     Sometimes her right fist flicked
or spasmed toward her face. For twelve hours
     until she died, he kept
scratching Jane Kenyon's big bony nose.
     A sharp, almost sweet
smell began to rise from her open mouth.
     He watched her chest go still.
With his thumb he closed her round brown eyes.

THOM GUNN

Lament

Your dying was a difficult enterprise.
First, petty things took up your energies,
The small but clustering duties of the sick,
Irritant as the cough's dry rhetoric.
Those hours of waiting for pills, shot, X-ray
Or test (while you read novels two a day)
Already with a kind of clumsy stealth
Distanced you from the habits of your health.
   In hope still, courteous still, but tired and thin,
You tried to stay the man that you had been,
Treating each symptom as a mere mishap
Without import. But then the spinal tap.
It brought a hard headache, and when night came
I heard you wake up from the same bad dream
Every half-hour with the same short cry
Of mild outrage, before immediately
Slipping into the nightmare once again
Empty of content but the drip of pain.
No respite followed: though the nightmare ceased,
Your cough grew thick and rich, its strength increased.
Four nights, and on the fifth we drove you down
To the Emergency Room. That frown, that frown:
I'd never seen such rage in you before
As when they wheeled you through the swinging door.
For you knew, rightly, they conveyed you from
Those normal pleasures of the sun's kingdom
The hedonistic body basks within
And takes for granted—summer on the skin,
Sleep without break, the moderate taste of tea
In a dry mouth. You had gone on from me
As if your body sought out martyrdom

In the far Canada of a hospital room.
Once there, you entered fully the distress
And long pale rigours of the wilderness.
A gust of morphine hid you. Back in sight
You breathed through a segmented tube, fat, white,
Jammed down your throat so that you could not speak.
  How thin the distance made you. In your cheek
One day, appeared the true shape of your bone
No longer padded. Still your mind, alone,
Explored this emptying intermediate
State for what holds and rests were hidden in it.
  You wrote us messages on a pad, amused
At one time that you had your nurse confused
Who, seeing you reconciled after four years
With your grey father, both of you in tears,
Asked if this was at last your 'special friend'
(The one you waited for until the end).
'She sings,' you wrote, 'a Philippine folk song
To wake me in the morning . . . It is long
And very pretty.' Grabbing at detail
To furnish this bare ledge toured by the gale,
On which you lay, bed restful as a knife,
You tried, tried hard, to make of it a life
Thick with the complicating circumstance
Your thoughts might fasten on. It had been chance
Always till now that had filled up the moment
With live specifics your hilarious comment
Discovered as it went along; and fed,
Laconic, quick, wherever it was led.
You improvised upon your own delight.
I think back to the scented summer night
We talked between our sleeping bags, below
A molten field of stars five years ago:
I was so tickled by your mind's light touch
I couldn't sleep, you made me laugh too much,
Though I was tired and begged you to leave off.

Now you were tired, and yet not tired enough
—Still hungry for the great world you were losing
Steadily in no season of your choosing—
And when at last the whole death was assured,
Drugs having failed, and when you had endured
Two weeks of an abominable constraint,
You faced it equably, without complaint,
Unwhimpering, but not at peace with it.
You'd lived as if your time was infinite:
You were not ready and not reconciled,
Feeling as uncompleted as a child
Till you had shown the world what you could do
In some ambitious role to be worked through,
A role your need for it had half-defined,
But never wholly, even in your mind.
You lacked the necessary ruthlessness,
The soaring meanness that pinpoints success.
We loved that lack of self-love, and your smile,
Rueful, at your own silliness.
                                    Meanwhile,
Your lungs collapsed, and the machine, unstrained,
Did all your breathing now. Nothing remained
But death by drowning on an inland sea
Of your own fluids, which it seemed could be
Kindly forestalled by drugs. Both could and would:
Nothing was said, everything understood,
At least by us. Your own concerns were not
Long-term, precisely, when they gave the shot
—You made local arrangements to the bed
And pulled a pillow round beside your head.
    And so you slept, and died, your skin gone grey,
Achieving your completeness, in a way.

Outdoors next day, I was dizzy from a sense
Of being ejected with some violence
From vigil in a white and distant spot

Where I was numb, into this garden plot
Too warm, too close, and not enough like pain.
I was delivered into time again
—The variations that I live among
Where your long body too used to belong
And where the still bush is minutely active.
You never thought your body was attractive,
Though others did, and yet you trusted it
And must have loved its fickleness a bit
Since it was yours and gave you what it could,
Till near the end it let you down for good,
Its blood hospitable to those guests who
Took over by betraying it into
The greatest of its inconsistencies
This difficult, tedious, painful enterprise.

ROY FISHER

As He Came Near Death

As he came near death things grew shallower for us:
We'd lost sleep and now sat muffled in the scent of tulips, the
                    medical odours, and the street sounds going past,
                    going away;
And he, too, slept little, the morphine and the pink light the
                    curtains let through floating him with us,
So that he lay and was worked out on to the skin of his life and
                    left there,
And we had to reach only a little way into the warm bed to scoop
                    him up.

A few days, slow tumbling escalators of visitors and cheques, and
                    something like popularity;
During this time somebody washed him in a soap called Narcissus
                    and mounted him, frilled with satin, in a polished
                    case.

Then the hole: this was a slot punched in a square of plastic grass
                    rug, a slot lined with white polythene, floored with
                    dyed green gravel.
The box lay in it; we rode in the black cars round a corner, got out
                    into our coloured cars and dispersed in easy stages.

After a time the grave got up and went away.

JOHN STONE

Death

I have seen   come on
slowly as rust
sand

or suddenly   as when
someone leaving
a room

finds the doorknob
come loose in his hand

FRANK BIDART

The Sacrifice

When Judas writes the history of SOLITUDE,—
. . . let him celebrate

Miss Mary Kenwood; who, without
help, placed her head in a plastic bag,

then locked herself
in a refrigerator.

—Six months earlier, after thirty years
teaching piano, she had watched

her mother slowly die of throat cancer.
Watched her *want* to die . . .

What once had given Mary life
in the end didn't want it.

Awake, her mother screamed for help to die.
—She felt

GUILTY . . . She knew that *all* men in these situations felt
innocent—; helpless—; yet guilty.

Christ knew the Secret. Betrayal
is necessary; as is woe for the betrayer.

The solution, Mary realized at last,
must be brought out of my own body.

Wiping away our sins, Christ stained us with his blood—;
to offer yourself, yet need *betrayal*, by *Judas*, before SHOULDERING

THE GUILT OF THE WORLD—;
... *Give me the courage not to need Judas.*

When Judas writes the history of solitude,
let him record

that to the friend who opened
the refrigerator, it seemed

death fought; before giving in.

DOUGLAS DUNN

Thirteen Steps and the Thirteenth of March

She sat up on her pillows, receiving guests.
I brought them tea or sherry like a butler,
Up and down the thirteen steps from my pantry.
I was running out of vases.

More than one visitor came down, and said,
"Her room's so cheerful. She isn't afraid."
Even the cyclamen and lilies were listening,
Their trusty tributes holding off the real.

Doorbells, shopping, laundry, post and callers,
And twenty-six steps up the stairs
From door to bed, two times thirteen's
Unlucky numeral in my high house.

And visitors, three, four, five times a day;
My wept exhaustions over plates and cups
Drained my self-pity in these days of grief
Before the grief. Flowers, and no vases left.

Tea, sherry, biscuits, cake, and whisky for the weak . . .
She fought death with an understated mischief—
"I suppose I'll have to make an effort"—
Turning down painkillers for lucidity.

Some sat downstairs with a hankie
Nursing a little cry before going up to her.
They came back with their fears of dying amended.
"Her room's so cheerful. She isn't afraid."

Each day was duty round the clock.
Our kissing conversations kept me going,
Those times together with the phone switched off,
Remembering our lives by candlelight.

John and Stuart brought their pictures round,
A travelling exhibition. Dying,
She thumbed down some, nodded at others,
An artist and curator to the last,

Honesty at all costs. She drew up lists,
Bequests, gave things away. It tore my heart out.
Her friends assisted at this tidying
In a conspiracy of women.

At night, I lay beside her in the unique hours.
There were mysteries in candle-shadows,
Birds, aeroplanes, the rabbits of our fingers,
The lovely, erotic flame of the candlelight.

Sad? Yes. But it was beautiful also.
There was a stillness in the world. Time was out
Walking his dog by the low walls and privet.
There was anonymity in words and music.

She wanted me to wear her wedding ring.
It wouldn't fit even my little finger.
It jammed on the knuckle. I knew why.
Her fingers dwindled and her rings slipped off.

After the funeral, I had them to tea and sherry
At the Newland Park. They said it was thoughtful.
I thought it was ironic — one last time —
A mad reprisal for their loyalty.

SHARON OLDS

The Lifting

Suddenly my father lifted up his nightie, I
turned my head away but he cried out
Shar!, my nickname, so I turned and looked.
He was sitting in the high cranked-up bed with the
gown up, around his neck,
to show me the weight he had lost. I looked
where his solid ruddy stomach had been
and I saw the skin fallen into loose
soft hairy rippled folds
lying in a pool of folds
down at the base of his abdomen,
the gaunt torso of a big man
who will die soon. Right away
I saw how much his hips are like mine,
the long, white angles, and then
how much his pelvis is shaped like my daughter's,
a chambered whelk-shell hollowed out,
I saw the folds of skin like something
poured, a thick batter, I saw
his rueful smile, the cast-up eyes as he
shows me his old body, he knows
I will be interested, he knows I will find him
appealing. If anyone had ever told me
I would sit by him and he would pull up his nightie
and I would look at him, at his naked body,
at the thick bud of his penis in all that
dark hair, look at him
in affection and uneasy wonder
I would not have believed it. But now I can still

see the tiny snowflakes, white and
night-blue, on the cotton of the gown as it
rises the way we were promised at death it would rise,
the veils would fall from our eyes, we would know everything.

LOUISE GLÜCK

Terminal Resemblance

When I saw my father for the last time, we both did the same thing.
He was standing in the doorway to the living room,
waiting for me to get off the telephone.
That he wasn't also pointing to his watch
was a signal he wanted to talk.

Talk for us always meant the same thing.
He'd say a few words. I'd say a few back.
That was about it.

It was the end of August, very hot, very humid.
Next door, workmen dumped new gravel on the driveway.

My father and I avoided being alone;
we didn't know how to connect, to make small talk—
there didn't seem to be
any other possibilities.
So this was special: when a man's dying,
he has a subject.

It must have been early morning. Up and down the street
sprinklers started coming on. The gardener's truck
appeared at the end of the block,
then stopped, parking.
My father wanted to tell me what it was like to be dying.
He told me he wasn't suffering.
He said he kept expecting pain, waiting for it, but it never came.
All he felt was a kind of weakness.
I said I was glad for him, that I thought he was lucky.

Some of the husbands were getting in their cars, going to work.
Not people we knew anymore. New families,
families with young children.
The wives stood on the steps, gesturing or calling.

We said goodbye in the usual way,
no embrace, nothing dramatic.
When the taxi came, my parents watched from the front door,
arm in arm, my mother blowing kisses as she always does,
because it frightens her when a hand isn't being used.
But for a change, my father didn't just stand there.
This time, he waved.

That's what I did, at the door to the taxi.
Like him, waved to disguise my hand's trembling.

PAUL MONETTE

No Goodbyes

for hours at the end I kissed your temple stroked
your hair and sniffed it it smelled so clean we'd
washed it Saturday night when the fever broke
as if there was always the perfect thing to do
to be alive for years I'd breathe your hair
when I came to bed late it was such pure you
why I nuzzle your brush every morning because
you're in there just like the dog the night
we unpacked the hospital bag and he skipped
and whimpered when Dad put on the red
sweater *Cover my bald spot will you*
you'd say and tilt your head like a parrot
so I could fix you up always always
till this one night when I was reduced to
I love you little friend here I am my
sweetest pea over and over spending all our
endearments like stray coins at a border
but wouldn't cry then no choked it because
they all said hearing was the last to go
the ear is like a wolf's till the very end
straining to hear a whole forest and I
wanted you loping off whatever you could
still dream to the sound of me at 3 P.M.
you were stable still our favorite word
at 4 you took the turn WAIT WAIT I AM
THE SENTRY HERE nothing passes as long as
I'm where I am we go on death is
a lonely hole two can leap it or else
or else there is nothing this man is mine
he's an ancient Greek like me I do
all the negotiating while he does battle

we are war and peace in a single bed
we wear the same size shirt it can't it can't
be yet not this just let me brush his hair
it's only Tuesday there's chicken in the fridge
from Sunday night he ate he slept oh why
don't all these kisses rouse you I won't won't
say it all I will say is goodnight patting
a few last strands in place you're covered now
my darling one last graze in the meadow
of you and please let your final dream be
a man not quite your size losing the whole
world but still here combing combing
singing your secret names till the night's gone

MARK DOTY

from Atlantis

6. NEW DOG

Jimi and Tony
can't keep Dino,
their cocker spaniel,
Tony's too sick,
the daily walks
more pressure
than pleasure,
one more obligation
that can't be met.

And though we already
have a dog, Wally
wants to adopt,
wants something small
and golden to sleep
next to him and
lick his face.
He's paralyzed now
from the waist down,

whatever's ruining him
moving upward, and
we don't know
how much longer
he'll be able to pet
a dog. How many men
want another attachment,
just as they're
leaving the world?

Wally sits up nights
and says, *I'd like*
some lizards, a talking bird,
some fish. A little rat.
So after I drive
to Jimi and Tony's
in the Village and they
meet me at the door and say,
We can't go through with it,

we can't give up our dog.
I drive to the shelter
—just to look—and there
is Beau: bounding and
practically boundless,
one brass concatenation
of tongue and tail,
unmediated energy,
too big, wild,

perfect. He not only
licks Wally's face
but bathes every
irreplaceable inch
of his head, and though
Wally can no longer
feed himself he can lift
his hand, and bring it
to rest on the rough gilt

flanks when they are,
for a moment, still.
I have never seen a touch
so deliberate.
It isn't about grasping;
the hand itself seems

almost blurred now,
softened, though
tentative only

because so much will
must be summoned,
such attention brought
to the work—which is all
he is now, this gesture
toward the restless splendor,
the unruly, the golden,
the animal, the new.

TOM SLEIGH

from The Work

6. THE CURRENT

The numbing current of the Demerol
Sweeps him out to sea where the secret night
He lives in slowly begins to darken,
His daytime routine of watching his blood cycle

Through the tubes of a machine shadowed by blackness
Blinding as an underwater cave. Already
He filters the dark water through gills aligned
To strain that element he more and more resembles:

Like walls of water held in miraculous
Suspension, the moment of his death looms impartially
Above him, my hand holding his tightening
Its grip even as his hand loosens . . .

As if my hand could lead him past that undulating
Weight towering above us out of sight.

RAFAEL CAMPO

from **Ten Patients, and Another**

V. JOHN DOE

An elderly white male, unresponsive.
Looks homeless. Maybe he's been here before:
No chart. No history. His vital signs
Were barely present, temperature was down
Near ninety, pressure ninety over palp;
The pulse was forty, best as they could tell.
They'll hook him to a monitor before
They warm him up. I didn't listen to
His lungs—I bet I'd hear a symphony
In there. I couldn't check his pupils since
His lids were frozen shut, but there were no
External signs of trauma to the head.
They found this picture of a woman with
Two tiny kids still pinned inside his coat.
It's only three A.M. The night's young. If
He's lucky, by tomorrow he'll be dead.

2.

"In the Chill of the Body":

Viewing the Dead

How does the body *mean* when life has left it? As the poems collected here suggest, poets find a range of messages in the seemingly empty materiality of death. To Tess Gallagher, who remembers her husband lying "in our house. / Three nights in the chill of the body" during the ritual interval of a wake, the "halo of cold" around her beloved hinted that "the body's messages carry farther / in death," while for William Carlos Williams a dead man is no more than "a godforsaken curio / without / any breath in it." Yet even a "curio" is a mystery, and so, whether (with Whitman) a poet sees a dead man as having a face like "the face of the Christ himself, / Dead and divine and brother of all," or whether (with Emily Dickinson) she defines the dead one as an "it" that is utterly alien (" 'Twas warm—at first—like Us— / Until there crept upon / A Chill" and "It crowded Cold to Cold—"), the abandoned body seems to many writers quite literally to incarnate a kind of ultimate enigma.

WALT WHITMAN

A Sight in Camp in the Daybreak Gray and Dim

A sight in camp in the daybreak gray and dim,
As from my tent I emerge so early sleepless.
As slow I walk in the cool fresh air the path near by the hospital tent,
Three forms I see on stretchers lying, brought out there untended
    lying,
Over each the blanket spread, ample brownish woolen blanket,
Gray and heavy blanket, folding, covering all.

Curious I halt and silent stand,
Then with light fingers I from the face of the nearest the first just lift
    the blanket;
Who are you elderly man so gaunt and grim, with well-gray'd hair, and
    flesh all sunken about the eyes?
Who are you my dear comrade?

Then to the second I step—and who are you my child and darling?
Who are you sweet boy with cheeks yet blooming?

Then to the third—a face nor child nor old, very calm, as a beautiful
    yellow-white ivory;
Young man I think I know you—I think this face is the face of the
    Christ himself,
Dead and divine and brother of all, and here again he lies.

EMILY DICKINSON

'Twas warm—at first (#614)

'Twas warm—at first—like Us—
Until there crept upon
A Chill—like frost upon a Glass—
Till all the scene—be gone.

The Forehead copied Stone—
The Fingers grew too cold
To ache—and like a Skater's Brook—
The busy eyes—congealed—

It straightened—that was all—
It crowded Cold to Cold—
It multiplied indifference—
As Pride were all it could—

And even when with Cords—
'Twas lowered, like a Weight—
It made no Signal, nor demurred,
But dropped like Adamant.

CHARLOTTE MEW

Beside the Bed

Someone has shut the shining eyes, straightened and folded
    The wandering hands quietly covering the unquiet breast:
So, smoothed and silenced you lie, like a child, not again to be
                        questioned or scolded;
    But, for you, not one of us believes that this is rest.

Not so to close the windows down can cloud and deaden
    The blue beyond: or to screen the wavering flame subdue its breath:
Why, if I lay my cheek to your cheek; your grey lips, like dawn, would
                        quiver and redden:
    Breaking into the old, odd smile at this fraud of death.

Because all night you have not turned to us or spoken
    It is time for you to wake; your dreams were never very deep:
I, for one, have seen the thin, bright, twisted threads of them dimmed
                        suddenly and broken;
    This is only a most piteous pretence of sleep!

ADELAIDE CRAPSEY

Triad

These be
Three silent things:
The falling snow . . . the hour
Before the dawn . . . the mouth of one
Just dead.

WALLACE STEVENS

The Emperor of Ice-Cream

Call the roller of big cigars,
The muscular one, and bid him whip
In kitchen cups concupiscent curds.
Let the wenches dawdle in such dress
As they are used to wear, and let the boys
Bring flowers in last month's newspapers.
Let be be finale of seem.
The only emperor is the emperor of ice-cream.

Take from the dresser of deal,
Lacking the three glass knobs, that sheet
On which she embroidered fantails once
And spread it so as to cover her face.
If her horny feet protrude, they come
To show how cold she is, and dumb.
Let the lamp affix its beam.
The only emperor is the emperor of ice-cream.

WILLIAM CARLOS WILLIAMS

Death

He's dead
the dog won't have to
sleep on his potatoes
any more to keep them
from freezing

he's dead
the old bastard—
He's a bastard because

there's nothing
legitimate in him any
more
       he's dead
He's sick-dead

               he's
a godforsaken curio
without
any breath in it

He's nothing at all
       he's dead
shrunken up to skin

      Put his head on
one chair and his
feet on another and
he'll lie there
like an acrobat—

Love's beaten. He
beat it. That's why
he's insufferable—

      because
he's here needing a
shave and making love
an inside howl
of anguish and defeat—

He's come out of the man
and he's let
the man go—
            the liar

Dead
      his eyes
rolled up out of
the light—a mockery

                which
love cannot touch—

just bury it
and hide its face
for shame.

D. H. LAWRENCE

The Bride

My love looks like a girl to-night,
  But she is old.
The plaits that lie along her pillow
  Are not gold,
But threaded with filigree silver,
  And uncanny cold.

She looks like a young maiden, since her brow
  Is smooth and fair,
Her cheeks are very smooth, her eyes are closed.
  She sleeps a rare
Still winsome sleep, so still, and so composed.

Nay, but she sleeps like a bride, and dreams her dreams
  Of perfect things.
She lies at last, the darling, in the shape of her dream,
  And her dead mouth sings
By its shape, like the thrushes in clear evenings.

EDNA ST. VINCENT MILLAY

from **Sonnets from an Ungrafted Tree**

XVII. GAZING UPON HIM NOW

Gazing upon him now, severe and dead,
It seemed a curious thing that she had lain
Beside him many a night in that cold bed,
And that had been which would not be again.
From his desirous body the great heat
Was gone at last, it seemed, and the taut nerves
Loosened forever. Formally the sheet
Set forth for her today those heavy curves
And lengths familiar as the bedroom door.
She was as one who enters, sly, and proud,
To where her husband speaks before a crowd,
And sees a man she never saw before —
The man who eats his victuals at her side,
Small, and absurd, and hers: for once, not hers, unclassified.

COUNTEE CULLEN

A Brown Girl Dead

With two white roses on her breasts,
    White candles at head and feet,
Dark Madonna of the grave she rests;
    Lord Death has found her sweet.

Her mother pawned her wedding ring
    To lay her out in white;
She'd be so proud she'd dance and sing
    To see herself tonight.

RUTH STONE

Habit

Every day I dig you up
And wipe off the rime
And look at you.
You are my joke,
My poem.
Your eyelids pull back from their sockets.
Your mouth mildews in scallops.
Worm filaments sprout from the pockets
Of your good suit.
I hold your sleeves in my arms;
Your waist drops a little putrid flesh.
I show you my old shy breasts.

W. D. SNODGRASS

Viewing the Body

Flowers like a gangster's funeral;
   Eyeshadow like a whore.
They all say isn't she beautiful.
   She, who never wore

Lipstick or such a dress,
   Never got taken out,
Was scarcely looked at, much less
   Wanted or talked about;

Who, gray as a mouse, crept
   The dark halls at her mother's
Or snuggled, soft, and slept
   Alone in the dim bedcovers.

Today at last she holds
   All eyes and a place of honor
Till the obscene red folds
   Of satin close down on her.

SYLVIA PLATH

Edge

The woman is perfected.
Her dead

Body wears the smile of accomplishment,
The illusion of a Greek necessity

Flows in the scrolls of her toga,
Her bare

Feet seem to be saying:
We have come so far, it is over.

Each dead child coiled, a white serpent,
One at each little

Pitcher of milk, now empty.
She has folded

Them back into her body as petals
Of a rose close when the garden

Stiffens and odors bleed
From the sweet, deep throats of the night flower.

The moon has nothing to be sad about,
Staring from her hood of bone.

She is used to this sort of thing.
Her blacks crackle and drag.

TONY HARRISON

Marked with D.

When the chilled dough of his flesh went in an oven
not unlike those he fuelled all his life,
I thought of his cataracts ablaze with Heaven
and radiant with the sight of his dead wife,
light streaming from his mouth to shape her name,
'not Florence and not Flo but always Florrie'.
I thought how his cold tongue burst into flame
but only literally, which makes me sorry,
sorry for his sake there's no Heaven to reach.
I get it all from Earth my daily bread
but he hungered for release from mortal speech
that kept him down, the tongue that weighed like lead.

The baker's man that no one will see rise
and England made to feel like some dull oaf
is smoke, enough to sting one person's eyes
and ash (not unlike flour) for one small loaf.

SHARON OLDS

His Ashes

The urn was heavy, small but so heavy,
like the time, weeks before he died,
when he needed to stand, I got my shoulder
under his armpit, my cheek against his
naked freckled warm back
while she held the urinal for him—he had
lost half his body weight
and yet he was so heavy we could hardly hold him up
while he got the fluid out crackling and
sputtering like a wet fire. The urn
had that six-foot heaviness, it began
to warm in my hands as I held it, under
the blue fir tree, stroking it.
The shovel got the last earth
out of the grave—it must have made that
kind of gritty iron noise when they
scraped his ashes out of the grate—
the others would be here any minute and I
wanted to open the urn as if then
I would finally know him. On the wet lawn,
under the cones cloaked in their rosin, I
worked at the top, it gave and slipped off and
there it was, the actual matter of his being:
small, speckled lumps of bone
like eggs; a discolored curve of bone like a
fungus grown around a branch;
spotted pebbles—and the spots were the channels of his marrow
where the live orbs of the molecules
swam as if by their own strong will
and in each cell the chromosomes
tensed and flashed, tore themselves

away from themselves, leaving their shining
duplicates. I looked at the jumble
of shards like a crushed paper-wasp hive:
was that a bone of his wrist, was that from the
elegant knee he bent, was that
his jaw, was that from his skull that at birth was
flexible yet—I looked at him,
bone and the ash it lay in, silvery
white as the shimmering coils of dust
the earth leaves behind it as it rolls, you can
hear its heavy roaring as it rolls away.

ELLEN BRYANT VOIGT

The Burial

Vermont, 1889

March, when the ground softened
and the men could dig the multiple graves,
was time enough to examine the winter's losses.
But the girl from Lower Cabot—
when they opened the coffins
to match the dead to their markers,
they found the corpse in terrific disarray:
bodice torn from the throat,
face sealed in distortion, eyes
open, the coins nowhere in evidence,
and in each fist a wad of her own dark hair.

TESS GALLAGHER

Wake

Three nights you lay in our house.
Three nights in the chill of the body.
Did I want to prove how surely
I'd been left behind? In the room's great dark
I climbed up beside you onto our high bed, bed
we'd loved in and slept in, married
and unmarried.

There was a halo of cold around you
as if the body's messages carry farther
in death, my own warmth taking on the silver-white
of a voice sent unbroken across snow just to hear
itself in its clarity of calling. We were dead
a little while together then, serene
and afloat on the strange broad canopy
of the abandoned world.

MOLLY PEACOCK

The Fare

Bury me in my pink pantsuit, you said—and I did.
But I'd never dressed you before! I saw the glint
of gold in your jewelry drawer and popped
the earrings in a plastic bag along with pearls,
a pink and gold pin, and your perfume. ("What's this?"
the mortician said . . . "Oh well, we'll spray some on.")
Now your words from the coffin: *Take my earrings off!*
I've had them on all day, for God's sake!
You've had them on five days. The lid's closed,
and the sharp stab of a femininity
you couldn't stand for more than two hours in life
is eternal—you'll never relax. I'm 400 miles away.
Should I call up the funeral home and have them removed?
You're not buried yet—stored till the ground thaws—
where, I didn't ask. Probably the mortician's garage.
I should have buried you in slippers and a bathrobe.
Instead, I gave them your shoes. Oh, please
do it for me. I can't stand the thought of you
pained by vanity forever. Reach your cold hand
up to your ear and pull and hear the click
of the clasp hinge unclasping, then reach
across your face and get the other one
and—this effort could take you days, I know,
since you're dead. Let it be your last effort:
to change my mistake and be dead in comfort.
Lower your hands in their places
on your low mound of stomach and rest, rest,
you can let go. They'll fall
to the bottom of the casket like tokens,
return fare fallen to the pit
of a coat's satin pocket.

MALENA MORLING

Ashes

Now the person you loved
the most in your whole life
Now the body
that held you
all night in bed
Now the arms
and the hands
Now the face that slept
against yours
the breath that moved
in and out of your mouth
Now the bright eyes
the forehead
the entire body
is lighter
than the flurries
that appear
out of nowhere

3.

"How to Perform a Funeral":

Ceremonies of Separation

"I will teach you my townspeople / how to perform a funeral—" begins William Carlos Williams's "Tract," arguably one of the twentieth century's profoundest yet most concise self-help manuals. A full-time practicing physician even while he forged a brilliant career as a modernist man of letters, Williams often had to watch beside the dying and comfort the bereaved, so he felt strongly the need for ceremonies of separation that would help the living bid farewell to the dead without cant or pomp but instead with sincerity and simplicity. Follow the hearse to the graveyard "with some show / of inconvenience; sit openly— / to the weather as to grief," Williams counseled mourners.

In their various ways most of the poets whose verses are included here have done what this wise physician-poet asked his townspeople to do. Whether, with Theodore Roethke, they feel nostalgia for solemn "pallbearers momentously taking their places" in traditional funeral processions, whether with Gwendolyn Brooks they long for a spiritual "sweet chariot" to "swing low swing low," or whether with Judi Benson they simply "unravel in the wind" of their own sorrow as they stand outside a columbarium, all "sit openly" to grief's desolate weather as they perform the ritual of farewell that must everywhere follow a death.

EMILY DICKINSON

There's been a Death, in the Opposite House (#547)

There's been a Death, in the Opposite House,
As lately as Today—
I know it, by the numb look
Such Houses have—alway—

The Neighbors rustle in and out—
The Doctor—drives away—
A Window opens like a Pod—
Abrupt—mechanically—

Somebody flings a Mattress out—
The Children hurry by—
They wonder if it died—on that—
I used to—when a Boy—

The Minister—goes stiffly in—
As if the House were His—
And He owned all the Mourners—now—
And little Boys—besides—

And then the Milliner—and the Man
Of the Appalling Trade—
To take the measure of the House—

There'll be that Dark Parade—

Of Tassels—and of Coaches—soon—
It's easy as a Sign—
The Intuition of the News—
In just a Country Town—

WILLIAM CARLOS WILLIAMS

Tract

I will teach you my townspeople
how to perform a funeral—
for you have it over a troop
of artists—
unless one should scour the world—
you have the ground sense necessary.
See! the hearse leads.
I begin with a design for a hearse.
For Christ's sake not black—
nor white either—and not polished!
Let it be weathered—like a farm wagon—
with gilt wheels (this could be
applied fresh at small expense)
or no wheels at all:
a rough dray to drag over the ground.

Knock the glass out!
My God—glass, my townspeople!
For what purpose? Is it for the dead
to look out or for us to see
how well he is housed or to see
the flowers or the lack of them—
or what?
To keep the rain and snow from him?
He will have a heavier rain soon:
pebbles and dirt and what not.
Let there be no glass—
and no upholstery, phew!
and no little brass rollers
and small easy wheels on the bottom—
my townspeople what are you thinking of?

A rough plain hearse then
with gilt wheels and no top at all.
On this the coffin lies
by its own weight.

                        No wreaths please—
especially no hot house flowers.
Some common memento is better,
something he prized and is known by:
his old clothes—a few books perhaps—
God knows what! You realize
how we are about these things
my townspeople—
something will be found—anything
even flowers if he had come to that.
So much for the hearse.

For heaven's sake though see to the driver!
Take off the silk hat! In fact
that's no place at all for him—
up there unceremoniously
dragging our friend out to his own dignity!
Bring him down—bring him down!
Low and inconspicuous! I'd not have him ride
on the wagon at all—damn him—
the undertaker's understrapper!
Let him hold the reins
and walk at the side
and inconspicuously too!

Then briefly as to yourselves:
Walk behind—as they do in France,
seventh class, or if you ride
Hell take curtains! Go with some show
of inconvenience; sit openly—
to the weather as to grief.

Or do you think you can shut grief in?
What—from us? We who have perhaps
nothing to lose? Share with us
share with us—it will be money
in your pockets.
                    Go now
I think you are ready.

THEODORE ROETHKE

On the Road to Woodlawn

I miss the polished brass, the powerful black horses,
The drivers creaking the seats of the baroque hearses,
The high-piled floral offerings with sentimental verses,
The carriages reeking with varnish and stale perfume.

I miss the pallbearers momentously taking their places,
The undertaker's obsequious grimaces,
The craned necks, the mourners' anonymous faces,
—And the eyes, still vivid, looking up from a sunken room.

GWENDOLYN BROOKS

Of De Witt Williams on His Way to Lincoln Cemetery

He was born in Alabama.
He was bred in Illinois.
He was nothing but a
Plain black boy.

Swing low swing low sweet sweet chariot.
Nothing but a plain black boy.

Drive him past the Pool Hall.
Drive him past the Show.
Blind within his casket,
But maybe he will know.

Down through Forty-seventh Street:
Underneath the L,
And Northwest Corner, Prairie,
That he loved so well.

Don't forget the Dance Halls—
Warwick and Savoy,
Where he picked his women, where
He drank his liquid joy.

Born in Alabama.
Bred in Illinois.
He was nothing but a
Plain black boy.

Swing low swing low sweet sweet chariot.
Nothing but a plain black boy.

J. C. HALL

Twelve Minutes

The hearse comes up the road
With its funeral load

Sharp on the stroke of twelve.
I greet it myself,

Good-morning the head man
Who's brought the dead man.

I say we're four only.
Still, he won't be lonely.

Being next of kin
I'm the first one in

Behind the bearers,
The black mourning wearers.

(A quick thought appals:
What if one trips and falls?)

They lay him safely down,
The coffin a light brown.

Prayers begin. I sit
And let my mind admit

That screwed-down speechless thing
And how another spring

His spouse was carried here.
Now they're remarried here

And may be happier even
In the clean church of heaven.

We say the last amen.
A button's pressed and then

To canned funeral strains
His dear dead remains,

Eighty-four years gone by,
Sink with a whirring sigh.

I tip and say goodbye.

ANNE STEVENSON

Minister

We're going to need the minister
to help this heavy body into the ground.

But he won't dig the hole.
Others who are stronger and weaker will have to do that.
And he won't wipe his nose and his eyes.
Others who are weaker and stronger will have to do that.
And he won't bake cakes or take care of the kids—
women's work—anyway,
what would they do at a time like this
if they didn't do that?

No, we'll get the minister to come
and take care of the words.

He doesn't have to make them up.
He doesn't have to say them well.
He doesn't have to like them
so long as they agree to obey him.

We have to have the minister
so the words will know where to go.

Imagine them circling and circling
the confusing cemetery.
Imagine them roving the earth
without anywhere to rest.

STEPHEN DUNN

On the Death of a Colleague

She taught theater, so we gathered
in the theater.
We praised her voice, her knowledge,
how good she was
with *Godot* and just four months later
with *Gigi*.
She was fifty. The problem in the liver.
Each of us recalled
an incident in which she'd been kind
or witty.
I told about being unable to speak
from my diaphragm
and how she made me lie down, placed her hand
where the failure was
and showed me how to breathe.
But afterwards
I only could do it when I lay down
and that became a joke
between us, and I told it as my offering
to the audience.
I was on stage and I heard myself
wishing to be impressive.
Someone else spoke of her cats
and no one spoke
of her face or the last few parties.
The fact was
I had avoided her for months.

It was a student's turn to speak, a sophomore,
one of her actors.

She was a drunk, he said, often came to class
reeking.
Sometimes he couldn't look at her, the blotches,
the awful puffiness.
And yet she was a great teacher,
he loved her,
but thought someone should say
what everyone knew
because she didn't die by accident.

Everyone was crying. Everyone was crying and it
was almost over now.
The remaining speaker, an historian, said he'd cut
his speech short.
And the Chairman stood up as if by habit,
said something about loss
and thanked us for coming. None of us moved
except some students
to the student who'd spoken, and then others
moved to him, across dividers,
down aisles, to his side of the stage.

CAROL MUSKE

The Eulogy

The man in the black suit delivers a eulogy
each page he turns, turns
a page of light on the ceiling,

because death mimics us, mocking
the eye's cowardly flight
from the flower-covered coffin

to the framed photo of the bereaved, alive.
It is not night.
It is California.

There are hibiscus dropping
their veined shrouds
on the crushed-stone path outside.

A gold cuff link blazes
as the eulogist raises his hands.

Shadows alter the ceiling,
the readable text.
There are two ways to meet death,

he says. One fearful,
the other courageous.
One day purposeful, the next hopeless,

A young man died because he had sex.
The eulogist speaks of soldiers under fire,
the cowards and the heroes.

The woman next to me cannot stop
weeping. I can find no tears inside
me. The cuff links beam

signals at us, above us.
The sun through the skylight
grows brighter and brighter:

Watch now, God,
Watch the eulogist raise his hands.
The rays, like your lasers,

blind the front rows.
The gifts love gives us!
Some of us flinch, some do not.

JUDI BENSON

Columbarium

(in memory of my father Captain "Rags" Parish, 1905–95)

It's the misunderstanding of ashes at the airport,
confusion over containers at the Academy,
the solemnity, the familiar uniform;

It's the gun salute sending shock waves across the water,
the bugle playing *Taps*,
the presentation of the flag,
the young cadet's voice trembling;
It's the smooth leaded box slotted in,
sun glint on engraved wings,
the miniature blue and gold curtains closing—

that is my undoing.

I unravel in the wind,
so many bits of string without a kite.

MARY STEWART HAMMOND

from Blessings

3. PAYING RESPECTS

Our fourth night of being, her children
and I, alone in her house without her,
she was returned from the mainland
after hours for the cemetery, and so
her two sons collected her at the ferry
and brought her back for one last night,
setting her down on the cobbler's bench.
We ignored her as if she were there.
At her usual bedtime her elder son
carried the cardboard box into her room
and sat it in the middle of the made bed.

Both were early risers and before anyone
was up he slipped downstairs in his robe,
tucked the box in the crook of his arm,
and walked to the beach the way her legs
couldn't this last year, sitting on the steps
watching the water materialize. From there
he traveled all their conjoint projects
in her fifteen years of widowhood, over all
her earthly domain, bearing the ashes
around to the boathouse, off through marsh grass
to the pond to review the erosion, through
deep sand to the point and the ospreys' nest, on
to the new section cleared of bittersweet,
and back in the spreading light to the driveway,
the dormers over the garage, into the basement
to inspect the new hot water tank,
the settings for the lawn sprinkler system,

before walking, room by room, through her house,
each with its fading wallpaper from her own
mother's reign, lingering at the thresholds
of her sleeping middle-aged children, ending
in the parlor where she presided mornings,
putting the box down, while he went to dress,
on her place on the sofa. He omitted,
his sister was sure when she saw the box there,
the inflexible part of their mother's routine.
She scooped it up and ran, the vaguely
hostile son calling out, "Don't forget to put
the lid down first," both of them pouring cereal
giggling, fidgeting, hearing a burst of laughter
when he found her, both swooping off
to the john to join him, all three laughing,
leaning against the tiles, until they cried.

When it was time to leave for Tower Hill
we waited in the Buick trying not to see him
standing on the knoll with the box
taking a last look at Nantucket Sound,
trying not to see him, when he turned,
this gangling, aging boy and his Mamma,
offer his arm, trying not to see him,
bending slightly to her height and weight,
pat the place on his forearm and tuck it
close. At her pace, they proceeded
away from the sea to her English garden,
nodding and bowing in succession
to the zinnias, the marigolds, the roses,
the hollyhocks, bowing and bowing
to dahlias, asters, Marguerites, phlox,
thanking and thanking.

AGHA SHAHID ALI

Cremation

Your bones refused to burn
when we set fire to the flesh.

Who would have guessed
you'd be stubborn in death?

JOSEPH STROUD

Documentary

Bring the camera closer in. Focus
On the burning *ghat*. They've finished
The ceremony around the body, and are torching
The wooden pyre. See how the tongues of flame
Rise from the limbs. Zero in on the head—
I want you to catch the skull when it bursts.
Pan down the torso, the spine in ashes, the hips
Crumbling. Then dolly back for the scenic shot—
The Ganges flowing past. But keep the tension
Sharp, you might catch the silhouette
Of a river dolphin. Filter the lens
To bring the blue out of the mud-silt.
Now zoom down to the middle of the river,
That small boat, the boatman dumping a child
Overboard. Get his flex of muscle
As he struggles with the stone tied to the corpse.
Then back to the panorama, the vista. The storm
Rushing in. The lightning flashing far off
Over the river palace. The silver drizzle
Of rain. The quiet glow on the water.

CAROL ANN DUFFY

Funeral

Say milky cocoa we'd say,
you had the accent for it,
drunk you sometimes would. *Milky*

cocoa. Preston. We'd all
laugh. *Milky cocoa*. Drunk,
drunk. You laughed, saying it.

From all over the city
mourners swarmed, a demo against
death, into the cemetery.

You asked for nothing.
Three gravediggers, two minutes
of silence in the wind. Black

cars took us back. Serious
drinking. Awkward ghosts
getting the ale in. All afternoon

we said your name, repeated
the prayers of anecdotes,
bereaved and drunk

enough to think you might arrive,
say milky cocoa . . . Milky
cocoa, until we knew you'd gone.

4.

"Death, thou shalt die":

Imagining the Afterlife

More often than not, those who watch by the dying, as well as those who contemplate the body and bid farewell to the soul, are confounded by the cryptic absence into which what was so recently a warmly living presence seems to have vanished. Where do the dead go when, as William Butler Yeats puts it, "the ghost begins to quicken"? And how and why do they "go" there? And what (if anything) do they feel in that mysterious space?

Almost every culture around the world has evolved a set of responses, often highly elaborate ones, to these questions, while poets—from Homer to Dante, Milton, and a host of others—have furnished intricate visions of an afterlife led by departed spirits in the Greek Hades, the Hebrew Gan Eden, and the Christian Heaven or Hell, an afterlife in which, in John Donne's famous words, "One short sleep past, we wake eternally / And death shall be no more; Death, thou shalt die."

Among the visions of the afterlife included here, some are quite traditional, such as Henry Vaughan's confident claim that the dead whom he had loved "are all gone into the world of light!" or the certainty expressed in Sterling Brown's "Sister Lou" that

> Jesus will lead you
> To a room wid windows
> Openin' on cherry trees an' plum trees
> Bloomin' everlastin'.

Others, though, are more idiosyncratic, or more skeptical. Gwendolyn Brooks, for instance, imagines that a casket "can't hold" rebellious, vivacious "Cousin Vit," who stubbornly "rises in the sunshine" and goes "Back to the bars she knew and the repose / In love-rooms," while Thom Gunn wittily suggests that

> After their processing, the dead
> Sit down in groups and watch TV,

In which they must be interested,
For on it they see you and me.

More provisional, tentative, and doubtful, Jacqueline Osherow is perhaps
representative of many uncertain yet inventive poets at this millennial
moment. Contemplating "dust on the mantel," she speculates that it
may be at least in part the dust or ash of a human body. In that case, she
wonders, might such a collection of particles remember breath and
speech? And if so, she wonders further, "Who's to say it isn't listening
still?"

JOHN DONNE

from Holy Sonnets

X. DEATH, BE NOT PROUD

Death, be not proud, though some have callèd thee
Mighty and dreadful, for thou art not so;
For those whom thou think'st thou dost overthrow
Die not, poor Death, nor yet canst thou kill me.
From rest and sleep, which but thy pictures be,
Much pleasure; then from thee much more must flow,
And soonest our best men with thee do go,
Rest of their bones, and soul's delivery.
Thou art slave to fate, chance, kings, and desperate men,
And dost with poison, war, and sickness dwell,
And poppy or charms can make us sleep as well
And better than thy stroke; why swell'st thou then?
One short sleep past, we wake eternally
And death shall be no more; Death, thou shalt die.

HENRY VAUGHAN

They Are All Gone into the World of Light!

They are all gone into the world of light!
   And I alone sit ling'ring here;
Their very memory is fair and bright,
   And my sad thoughts doth clear.

It glows and glitters in my cloudy breast
   Like stars upon some gloomy grove,
Or those faint beams in which this hill is dressed
   After the sun's remove.

I see them walking in an air of glory,
   Whose light doth trample on my days;
My days, which are at best but dull and hoary,
   Mere glimmering and decays.

O holy hope, and high humility,
   High as the heavens above!
These are your walks, and you have showed them me
   To kindle my cold love.

Dear, beauteous death! the jewel of the just,
   Shining nowhere but in the dark;
What mysteries do lie beyond thy dust,
   Could man outlook that mark!

He that hath found some fledged bird's nest may know
   At first sight if the bird be flown;
But what fair well or grove he sings in now,
   That is to him unknown.

And yet, as angels in some brighter dreams
    Call to the soul when man doth sleep,
So some strange thoughts transcend our wonted themes,
    And into glory peep.

If a star were confined into a tomb,
    Her captive flames must needs burn there;
But when the hand that locked her up gives room,
    She'll shine through all the sphere.

O Father of eternal life, and all
    Created glories under thee!
Resume thy spirit from this world of thrall
    Into true liberty!

Either disperse these mists, which blot and fill
    My perspective still as they pass;
Or else remove me hence unto that hill
    Where I shall need no glass.

ALGERNON CHARLES SWINBURNE

The Garden of Proserpine

Here, where the world is quiet;
　　Here, where all trouble seems
Dead winds' and spent waves' riot
　　In doubtful dreams of dreams;
I watch the green field growing
For reaping folk and sowing,
For harvest time and mowing,
　　A sleepy world of streams.

I am tired of tears and laughter,
　　And men that laugh and weep;
Of what may come hereafter
　　For men that sow to reap;
I am weary of days and hours,
Blown buds of barren flowers,
Desires and dreams and powers
　　And everything but sleep.

Here life has death for neighbor,
　　And far from eye or ear
Wan waves and wet winds labor,
　　Weak ships and spirits steer;
They drive adrift, and whither
They wot not who make thither;
But no such winds blow hither,
　　And no such things grow here.

No growth of moor or coppice,
　　No heather flower or vine,
But bloomless buds of poppies,
　　Green grapes of Proserpine,

Pale beds of blowing rushes,
Where no leaf blooms or blushes
Save this whereout she crushes
    For dead men deadly wine.

Pale, without name or number,
    In fruitless fields of corn,
They bow themselves and slumber
    All night till light is born;
And like a soul belated,
In hell and heaven unmated,
By cloud and mist abated
    Comes out of darkness morn.

Though one were strong as seven,
    He too with death shall dwell,
Nor wake with wings in heaven,
    Nor weep for pains in hell;
Though one were fair as roses,
His beauty clouds and closes;
And well though love reposes,
    In the end it is not well.

Pale, beyond porch and portal,
    Crowned with calm leaves, she stands
Who gathers all things mortal
    With cold immortal hands;
Her languid lips are sweeter
Than love's who fears to greet her
To men that mix and meet her
    From many times and lands.

She waits for each and other,
    She waits for all men born;
Forgets the earth her mother,
    The life of fruits and corn;

And spring and seed and swallow
Take wing for her and follow
Where summer song rings hollow
    And flowers are put to scorn.

There go the loves that wither,
    The old loves with wearier wings;
And all dead years draw thither,
    And all disastrous things;
Dead dreams of days forsaken,
Blind buds that snows have shaken,
Wild leaves that winds have taken,
    Red strays of ruined springs.

We are not sure of sorrow,
    And joy was never sure;
Today will die tomorrow;
    Time stoops to no man's lure;
And love, grown faint and fretful,
With lips but half regretful
Sighs, and with eyes forgetful
    Weeps that no loves endure.

From too much love of living,
    From hope and fear set free,
We thank with brief thanksgiving
    Whatever gods may be
That no life lives forever;
That dead men rise up never;
That even the weariest river
    Winds somewhere safe to sea.

Then star nor sun shall waken,
    Nor any change of light:
Nor sound of waters shaken,
    Nor any sound or sight:

Nor wintry leaves nor vernal,
Nor days nor things diurnal;
Only the sleep eternal
    In an eternal night.

WILLIAM BUTLER YEATS

The Cold Heaven

Suddenly I saw the cold and rook-delighting Heaven
That seemed as though ice burned and was but the more ice,
And thereupon imagination and heart were driven
So wild that every casual thought of that and this
Vanished, and left but memories, that should be out of season
With the hot blood of youth, of love crossed long ago;
And I took all the blame out of all sense and reason,
Until I cried and trembled and rocked to and fro,
Riddled with light. Ah! when the ghost begins to quicken,
Confusion of the death-bed over, is it sent
Out naked on the roads, as the books say, and stricken
By the injustice of the skies for punishment?

STERLING A. BROWN

Sister Lou

Honey
When de man
Calls out de las' train
You're gonna ride,
Tell him howdy.

Gather up yo' basket
An' yo' knittin' an' yo' things,
An' go on up an' visit
Wid frien' Jesus fo' a spell.

Show Marfa
How to make yo' greengrape jellies,
An' give po' Lazarus
A passel of them Golden Biscuits.

Scald some meal
Fo' some rightdown good spoonbread
Fo' li'l box-plunkin' David.

An' sit aroun'
An' tell them Hebrew Chillen
All yo' stories. . . .

Honey
Don't be feared of them pearly gates,
Don't go 'round to de back,
No mo' dataway
Not evah no mo'.

Let Michael tote yo' burden
An' yo' pocketbook an' evahthing

'Cept yo' Bible,
While Gabriel blows somp'n
Solemn but loudsome
On dat horn of his'n.

Honey
Go straight on to de Big House,
An' speak to yo' God
Widout no fear an' tremblin'.

Then sit down
An' pass de time of day awhile.

Give a good talkin' to
To yo' favorite 'postle Peter,
An' rub the po' head
Of mixed-up Judas,
An' joke awhile wid Jonah.

Then, when you gits de chance,
Always rememberin' yo' raisin',
Let 'em know youse tired
Jest a mite tired.

Jesus will find yo' bed fo' you
Won't no servant evah bother wid yo' room.
Jesus will lead you
To a room wid windows
Openin' on cherry trees an' plum trees
Bloomin' everlastin'.

An' dat will be yours
Fo' keeps.

Den take yo' time. . . .
Honey, take yo' bressed time.

GWENDOLYN BROOKS

The Rites for Cousin Vit

Carried her unprotesting out the door.
Kicked back the casket-stand. But it can't hold her,
That stuff and satin aiming to enfold her,
The lid's contrition nor the bolts before.
Oh oh. Too much. Too much. Even now, surmise,
She rises in the sunshine. There she goes,
Back to the bars she knew and the repose
In love-rooms and the things in people's eyes.
Too vital and too squeaking. Must emerge.
Even now she does the snake-hips with a hiss,
Slops the bad wine across her shantung, talks
Of pregnancy, guitars and bridgework, walks
In parks or alleys, comes haply on the verge
Of happiness, haply hysterics. Is.

PHILIP LARKIN

The Explosion

On the day of the explosion
Shadows pointed towards the pithead:
In the sun the slagheap slept.

Down the lane came men in pitboots
Coughing oath-edged talk and pipe-smoke,
Shouldering off the freshened silence.

One chased after rabbits; lost them;
Came back with a nest of lark's eggs;
Showed them; lodged them in the grasses.

So they passed in beards and moleskins,
Fathers, brothers, nicknames, laughter,
Through the tall gates standing open.

At noon, there came a tremor; cows
Stopped chewing for a second; sun,
Scarfed as in a heat-haze, dimmed.

The dead go on before us, they
Are sitting in God's house in comfort,
We shall see them face to face—

Plain as lettering in the chapels
It was said, and for a second
Wives saw men of the explosion

Larger than in life they managed—
Gold as on a coin, or walking
Somehow from the sun towards them,

One showing the eggs unbroken.

JAMES DICKEY

The Heaven of Animals

Here they are. The soft eyes open.
If they have lived in a wood
It is a wood.
If they have lived on plains
It is grass rolling
Under their feet forever.

Having no souls, they have come,
Anyway, beyond their knowing.
Their instincts wholly bloom
And they rise.
The soft eyes open.

To match them, the landscape flowers,
Outdoing, desperately
Outdoing what is required:
The richest wood,
The deepest field.

For some of these,
It is, without blood.
These hunt, as they have done,
But with claws and teeth grown perfect,

More deadly than they can believe.
They stalk more silently,
And crouch on the limbs of trees,
And their descent
Upon the bright backs of their prey

May take years
In a sovereign floating of joy.
And those that are hunted
Know this as their life,
Their reward: to walk

Under such trees in full knowledge
Of what is in glory above them,
And to feel no fear,
But acceptance, compliance.
Fulfilling themselves without pain

At the cycle's center,
They tremble, they walk
Under the tree,
They fall, they are torn,
They rise, they walk again.

ANNE SEXTON

Somewhere in Africa

Must you leave, John Holmes, with the prayers and psalms
you never said, said over you? Death with no rage
to weigh you down? Praised by the mild God, his arm
over the pulpit, leaving you timid, with no real age,

whitewashed by belief, as dull as the windy preacher!
Dead of a dark thing, John Holmes, you've been lost
in the college chapel, mourned as father and teacher,
mourned with piety and grace under the University Cross.

Your last book unsung, your last hard words unknown,
abandoned by science, cancer blossomed in your throat,
rooted like bougainvillea into your gray backbone,
ruptured your pores until you wore it like a coat.

The thick petals, the exotic reds, the purples and whites
covered up your nakedness and bore you up with all
their blind power. I think of your last June nights
in Boston, your body swollen but light, your eyes small

as you let the nurses carry you into a strange land.
. . . If this is death and God is necessary let him be hidden
from the missionary, the well-wisher and the glad hand.
Let God be some tribal female who is known but forbidden.

Let there be this God who is a woman who will place you
upon her shallow boat, who is a woman naked to the waist,
moist with palm oil and sweat, a woman of some virtue
and wild breasts, her limbs excellent, unbruised and chaste.

Let her take you. She will put twelve strong men at the oars
for you are stronger than mahogany and your bones fill
the boat high as with fruit and bark from the interior.
She will have you now, you whom the funeral cannot kill.

John Holmes, cut from a single tree, lie heavy in her hold
and go down that river with the ivory, the copra and the gold.

THOM GUNN

Death's Door

Of course the dead outnumber us
— How their recruiting armies grow!
My mother archaic now as Minos,
She who died forty years ago.

After their processing, the dead
Sit down in groups and watch TV,
In which they must be interested,
For on it they see you and me.

These four, who though they never met
Died in one month, sit side by side
Together in front of the same set,
And all without a *TV Guide*.

Arms round each other's shoulders loosely,
Although they can feel nothing, who
When they unlearned their pain so sprucely
Let go of all sensation too.

Thus they watch friend and relative
And life here as they think it is
— In black and white, repetitive
As situation comedies.

With both delight and tears at first
They greet each programme on death's stations,
But in the end lose interest,
Their boredom turning to impatience.

'He misses me? He must be kidding
—This week he's sleeping with a cop.'
'All she reads now is *Little Gidding*.'
'They're getting old. I wish they'd stop.'

The habit of companionship
Lapses—they break themselves of touch:
Edging apart at arm and hip,
Till separated on the couch,

They woo amnesia, look away
As if they were not yet elsewhere,
And when snow blurs the picture they,
Turned, give it a belonging stare.

Snow blows out toward them, till their seat
Filling with flakes becomes instead
Snow-bank, snow-landscape, and in that
They find themselves with all the dead,

Where passive light from snow-crust shows them
Both Minos circling and my mother.
Yet none of the recruits now knows them,
Nor do they recognize each other,

They have been so superbly trained
Into the perfect discipline
Of an archaic host, and weaned
From memory briefly barracked in.

SANDRA M. GILBERT

November 26, 1992: Thanksgiving at the Sea Ranch, Contemplating Metempsychosis

You tried coming back as a spider.
I was too fast for you. As you
climbed my ankle, I swept you off, I ground you

to powder under my winter boot.
Shall I cherish the black widow,
I asked, because he is you?

You were cunning: you became
the young, the darkly masked
raccoon that haunts my deck.

Each night for weeks you tiptoed
toward the sliding doors, your paws
imploring, eyes aglow. *Let me in,*

Let me back in, you hissed,
swaying beside the tubbed fuchsia,
shadowing the fancy cabbage in its Aztec pot.

And you've been creatures of the air and sea,
the hawk that sees into my skull, the seal that barks
a few yards from the picnic on the shore.

Today you chose a different life, today
you're trying to stumble
through the tons of dirt that hold you down:

you're a little grove of mushrooms,
rising from the forest floor you loved.
Bob saw you in the windbreak—

November mushrooms, he said,
off-white and probably poisonous.
Shall I slice you for the feast?

If I eat you will I die back into your arms?
Shall I give thanks for God's wonders
because they all are you, and you are them?

The meadow's silent, its dead grasses
ignore each other and the evening walkers
who trample them. What will you be,

I wonder, when the night wind rises?
Come back as yourself, in your blue parka,
your plaid flannel shirt with the missing button.

These fields that hum and churn with life
are empty. There is nowhere
you are not, nowhere

you are not not.

ALICE WALKER

"Good Night, Willie Lee, I'll See You in the Morning"

Looking down into my father's
dead face
for the last time
my mother said without
tears, without smiles
without regrets
but with *civility*
"Good night, Willie Lee, I'll see you
in the morning."
And it was then I knew that the healing
of all our wounds
is forgiveness
that permits a promise
of our return
at the end.

ELLERY AKERS

The Dead

The dead come, looking for their shoes.
It's all right if we can't find them:
it was only the dark, inside, they wanted.
It's all right. They can be the shadow of a boulder,
or the oak leaves falling, one by one.
There have been so many of them, and so few of us.
The ones we loved take our hands in the morning
and watch us:
Eyes in the river.
One day we will be like them,
and rise, like waves, out of the hot fields.

JACQUELINE OSHEROW

Dust on the Mantel: Sonnet

I wonder if the dust collecting here
Remembers breath, how it, too, used to waste
Hours seeming to study the empty air,
Perfecting—or so it thought—the art of daydream
On passersby, weather, cars, stray leaves
As if wholly unsuspecting that a person lives
And dies. How it could talk on the phone,
Watch movies, flip through magazines, this dust.
It even undertook to write a poem
After it settled on a book opened to one
That made a fleeting afternoon stand still.
It braced itself to overhear a voice
Murmur something unequivocally precious.
Who's to say it isn't listening still?

II.

Grieving:

Lamentations

for the Dead

1.

"Begin then, Sisters of the Sacred Well":

The Pastoral Tradition

Among the most powerful and influential verse lamentations that western culture has produced are poems of mourning in the specialized genre known as the "pastoral elegy." Of these, the two most famous examples written in English are certainly John Milton's "Lycidas" and Percy Bysshe Shelley's "Adonais." Like all pastoral elegies, these poems are purportedly spoken by and about shepherds—the Greek word for "shepherd" is *pastor*—but the "pastoral" or rural world of these literary shepherds is a magical realm peopled not only by simple country folk but also by nymphs and muses, fauns and satyrs, even ancient Greek or Roman gods and goddesses.

Such fanciful, highly stylized settings and conventions, however, ultimately help intensify the ritual expressions of grief that Milton and Shelley offer in tribute to the dead friends for whom they mourn. Milton's poem was written in memory of a college associate, Edward King, who drowned in an accident at sea in 1637, while Shelley's was composed to elegize the great Romantic poet John Keats, who died of tuberculosis in 1821, at the early age of twenty-five. Yet because the exigencies of the form compel the two authors to transform the particular persons known in life as Edward King and John Keats into the mythical dead shepherd-poets "Lycidas" and "Adonais," the two dead men become, in a sense, universal figures who represent all the human treasure lost when life is cut off too soon. Richly imagined and majestically versified, the works that lament their early deaths have profoundly affected the tradition of the English-language elegy. In one way or another, indeed, most poets who have crafted formal elegies in the last few centuries have learned from these texts, with some seeking to recapture Milton's or Shelley's solemnity in their own words, and others striving to construct new and different modes of mourning.

JOHN MILTON

Lycidas

In this monody the author bewails a learned friend, unfortunately drowned in his passage from Chester on the Irish Seas, 1637. And by occasion foretells the ruin of our corrupted clergy, then in their height.

    Yet once more, O ye laurels, and once more
Ye myrtles brown, with ivy never sere,
I come to pluck your berries harsh and crude,
And with forced fingers rude,
Shatter your leaves before the mellowing year.
Bitter constraint, and sad occasion dear,
Compels me to disturb your season due;
For Lycidas is dead, dead ere his prime,
Young Lycidas, and hath not left his peer.
Who would not sing for Lycidas? He knew
Himself to sing, and build the lofty rhyme.
He must not float upon his watery bier
Unwept, and welter to the parching wind,
Without the meed of some melodious tear.
    Begin then, sisters of the sacred well
That from beneath the seat of Jove doth spring,
Begin, and somewhat loudly sweep the string.
Hence with denial vain, and coy excuse;
So may some gentle Muse
With lucky words favor my destined urn,
And as he passes turn,
And bid fair peace be to my sable shroud.
For we were nursed upon the selfsame hill,
Fed the same flock, by fountain, shade, and rill.
    Together both, ere the high lawns appeared
Under the opening eyelids of the morn,
We drove afield, and both together heard

What time the grayfly winds her sultry horn,
Battening our flocks with the fresh dews of night,
Oft till the star that rose at evening bright
Toward heaven's descent had sloped his westering wheel.
Meanwhile the rural ditties were not mute,
Tempered to th' oaten flute,
Rough satyrs danced, and fauns with cloven heel
From the glad sound would not be absent long,
And old Damoetas loved to hear our song.
　　But O the heavy change, now thou art gone,
Now thou art gone, and never must return!
Thee, shepherd, thee the woods and desert caves,
With wild thyme and the gadding vine o'ergrown,
And all their echoes mourn.
The willows and the hazel copses green
Shall now no more be seen,
Fanning their joyous leaves to thy soft lays.
As killing as the canker to the rose,
Or taint-worm to the weanling herds that graze,
Or frost to flowers that their gay wardrobe wear
When first the white-thorn blows;
Such, Lycidas, thy loss to shepherd's ear.
　　Where were ye, nymphs, when the remorseless deep
Closed o'er the head of your loved Lycidas?
For neither were ye playing on the steep
Where your old bards, the famous Druids, lie,
Nor on the shaggy top of Mona high,
Nor yet where Deva spreads her wizard stream:
Ay me! I fondly dream—
Had ye been there—for what could that have done?
What could the Muse herself that Orpheus bore,
The Muse herself, for her inchanting son
Whom universal Nature did lament,
When by the rout that made the hideous roar
His gory visage down the stream was sent,
Down the swift Hebrus to the Lesbian shore?

Alas! What boots it with incessant care
To tend the homely slighted shepherd's trade,
And strictly meditate the thankless Muse?
Were it not better done as others use,
To sport with Amaryllis in the shade,
Or with the tangles of Neaera's hair?
Fame is the spur that the clear spirit doth raise
(That last infirmity of noble mind)
To scorn delights, and live laborious days;
But the fair guerdon when we hope to find,
And think to burst out into sudden blaze,
Comes the blind Fury with th' abhorrèd shears,
And slits the thin-spun life. "But not the praise,"
Phoebus replied, and touched my trembling ears;
"Fame is no plant that grows on mortal soil,
Nor in the glistering foil
Set off to th' world, nor in broad rumor lies,
But lives and spreads aloft by those pure eyes,
And perfect witness of all-judging Jove;
As he pronounces lastly on each deed,
Of so much fame in heaven expect thy meed."
    O fountain Arethuse, and thou honored flood,
Smooth-sliding Mincius, crowned with vocal reeds,
That strain I heard was of a higher mood.
But now my oat proceeds,
And listens to the herald of the sea
That came in Neptune's plea.
He asked the waves, and asked the felon winds,
"What hard mishap hath doomed this gentle swain?"
And questioned every gust of rugged wings
That blows from off each beakèd promontory;
They knew not of his story,
And sage Hippotades their answer brings,
That not a blast was from his dungeon strayed;
The air was calm, and on the level brine,
Sleek Panope with all her sisters played.

It was that fatal and perfidious bark,
Built in th' eclipse, and rigged with curses dark,
That sunk so low that sacred head of thine.
   Next Camus, reverend sire, went footing slow,
His mantle hairy, and his bonnet sedge,
Inwrought with figures dim, and on the edge
Like to that sanguine flower inscribed with woe.
"Ah! who hath reft," quoth he, "my dearest pledge?"
Last came and last did go
The pilot of the Galilean lake;
Two massy keys he bore of metals twain
(The golden opes, the iron shuts amain).
He shook his mitered locks, and stern bespake:
"How well could I have spared for thee, young swain,
Enow of such as for their bellies' sake
Creep and intrude and climb into the fold!
Of other care they little reckoning make,
Than how to scramble at the shearers' feast,
And shove away the worthy bidden guest.
Blind mouths! that scarce themselves know how to hold
A sheep-hook, or have learned aught else the least
That to the faithful herdsman's art belongs!
What recks it them? What need they? They are sped;
And when they list, their lean and flashy songs
Grate on their scrannel pipes of wretched straw.
The hungry sheep look up, and are not fed,
But swoln with wind, and the rank mist they draw,
Rot inwardly, and foul contagion spread,
Besides what the grim wolf with privy paw
Daily devours apace, and nothing said.
But that two-handed engine at the door
Stands ready to smite once, and smite no more."
   Return, Alpheus, the dread voice is past,
That shrunk thy streams; return, Sicilian muse,
And call the vales, and bid them hither cast
Their bells and flowerets of a thousand hues.

Ye valleys low where the mild whispers use,
Of shades and wanton winds, and gushing brooks,
On whose fresh lap the swart star sparely looks,
Throw hither all your quaint enameled eyes,
That on the green turf suck the honeyed showers,
And purple all the ground with vernal flowers.
Bring the rathe primrose that forsaken dies,
The tufted crow-toe, and pale jessamine,
The white pink, and the pansy freaked with jet,
The glowing violet,
The musk-rose, and the well-attired woodbine,
With cowslips wan that hang the pensive head,
And every flower that sad embroidery wears:
Bid amaranthus all his beauty shed,
And daffadillies fill their cups with tears,
To strew the laureate hearse where Lycid lies.
For so to interpose a little ease,
Let our frail thoughts dally with false surmise.
Ay me! whilst thee the shores and sounding seas
Wash far away, where'er thy bones are hurled,
Whether beyond the stormy Hebrides,
Where thou perhaps under the whelming tide
Visit'st the bottom of the monstrous world;
Or whether thou, to our moist vows denied,
Sleep'st by the fable of Bellerus old,
Where the great vision of the guarded mount
Looks toward Namancos and Bayona's hold;
Look homeward angel now, and melt with ruth:
And, O ye dolphins, waft the hapless youth.
    Weep no more, woeful shepherds, weep no more,
For Lycidas your sorrow is not dead.
Sunk though he be beneath the wat'ry floor;
So sinks the day-star in the ocean bed,
And yet anon repairs his drooping head,
And tricks his beams, and with new-spangled ore
Flames in the forehead of the morning sky:

So Lycidas sunk low, but mounted high,
Through the dear might of him that walked the waves,
Where, other groves and other streams along,
With nectar pure his oozy locks he laves,
And hears the unexpressive nuptial song,
In the blest kingdoms meek of joy and love.
There entertain him all the saints above,
In solemn troops and sweet societies
That sing, and singing in their glory move,
And wipe the tears forever from his eyes.
Now, Lycidas, the shepherds weep no more;
Henceforth thou art the genius of the shore,
In thy large recompense, and shalt be good
To all that wander in that perilous flood.
    Thus sang the uncouth swain to th' oaks and rills,
While the still morn went out with sandals gray;
He touched the tender stops of various quills,
With eager thought warbling his Doric lay:
And now the sun had stretched out all the hills,
And now was dropped into the western bay;
At last he rose, and twitched his mantle blue:
Tomorrow to fresh woods, and pastures new.

PERCY BYSSHE SHELLEY

Adonais

An Elegy on the Death of John Keats, Author of Endymion, Hyperion, etc.
[*Thou wert the morning star among the living.*
Ere thy fair light had fled—
Now, having died, thou art as Hesperus, giving
New splendour to the dead.]

1

    I weep for Adonais—he is dead!
    O, weep for Adonais! though our tears
    Thaw not the frost which binds so dear a head!
    And thou, sad Hour, selected from all years
    To mourn our loss, rouse thy obscure compeers,
    And teach them thine own sorrow, say: with me
    Died Adonais; till the Future dares
    Forget the Past, his fate and fame shall be
An echo and a light unto eternity!

2

    Where wert thou mighty Mother when he lay,
    When thy Son lay, pierced by the shaft which flies
    In darkness? where was lorn Urania
    When Adonais died? With veiled eyes,
    'Mid listening Echoes, in her Paradise
    She sate, while one, with soft enamoured breath,
    Rekindled all the fading melodies,
    With which, like flowers that mock the corse beneath,
He had adorned and hid the coming bulk of death.

3

O, weep for Adonais—he is dead!
Wake, melancholy Mother, wake and weep!
Yet wherefore? Quench within their burning bed
Thy fiery tears, and let thy loud heart keep
Like his, a mute and uncomplaining sleep;
For he is gone, where all things wise and fair
Descend;—oh, dream not that the amorous Deep
Will yet restore him to the vital air;
Death feeds on his mute voice, and laughs at our despair.

4

Most musical of mourners, weep again!
Lament anew, Urania!—He died,
Who was the Sire of an immortal strain,
Blind, old, and lonely, when his country's pride,
The priest, the slave, and the liberticide,
Trampled and mocked with many a loathed rite
Of lust and blood; he went, unterrified,
Into the gulph of death; but his clear Sprite
Yet reigns o'er earth; the third among the sons of light.

5

Most musical of mourners, weep anew!
Not all to that bright station dared to climb;
And happier they their happiness who knew,
Whose tapers yet burn through that night of time
In which suns perished; others more sublime,
Struck by the envious wrath of man or God,
Have sunk, extinct in their refulgent prime;
And some yet live, treading the thorny road,
Which leads, through toil and hate, to Fame's serene abode.

6

But now, thy youngest, dearest one, has perished—
The nursling of thy widowhood, who grew,
Like a pale flower by some sad maiden cherished,
And fed with true love tears, instead of dew;
Most musical of mourners, weep anew!
Thy extreme hope, the loveliest and the last,
The bloom, whose petals nipt before they blew
Died on the promise of the fruit, is waste;
The broken lily lies—the storm is overpast.

7

To that high Capital, where kingly Death
Keeps his pale court in beauty and decay,
He came; and bought, with price of purest breath,
A grave among the eternal.—Come away!
Haste, while the vault of blue Italian day
Is yet his fitting charnel-roof! while still
He lies, as if in dewy sleep he lay;
Awake him not! surely he takes his fill
Of deep and liquid rest, forgetful of all ill.

8

He will awake no more, oh, never more!—
Within the twilight chamber spreads apace,
The shadow of white Death, and at the door
Invisible Corruption waits to trace
His extreme way to her dim dwelling-place;
The eternal Hunger sits, but pity and awe
Soothe her pale rage, nor dares she to deface
So fair a prey, till darkness, and the law
Of change, shall 'oer his sleep the mortal curtain draw.

9

O, weep for Adonais! — The quick Dreams,
The passion-winged Ministers of thought,
Who were his flocks, whom near the living streams
Of his young spirit he fed, and whom he taught
The love which was its music, wander not, —
Wander no more, from kindling brain to brain,
But droop there, whence they sprung; and mourn their lot
Round the cold heart, where, after their sweet pain,
They ne'er will gather strength, or find a home again.

10

And one with trembling hands clasps his cold head,
And fans him with her moonlight wings, and cries;
"Our love, our hope, our sorrow, is not dead;
See, on the silken fringe of his faint eyes,
Like dew upon a sleeping flower, there lies
A tear some Dream has loosened from his brain."
Lost Angel of a ruined Paradise!
She knew not 'twas her own; as with no stain
She faded, like a cloud which had outwept its rain.

11

One from a lucid urn of starry dew
Washed his light limbs as if embalming them;
Another clipt her profuse locks, and threw
The wreath upon him, like an anadem,
Which frozen tears instead of pearls begem;
Another in her wilful grief would break
Her bow and winged reeds, as if to stem
A greater loss with one which was more weak;
And dull the barbed fire against his frozen cheek.

12

Another Splendour on his mouth alit,
That mouth, whence it was wont to draw the breath
Which gave it strength to pierce the guarded wit,
And pass into the panting heart beneath
With lightning and with music: the damp death
Quenched its caress upon his icy lips;
And, as a dying meteor stains a wreath
Of moonlight vapour, which the cold night clips,
It flushed through his pale limbs, and past to its eclipse.

13

And others came . . . Desires and Adorations,
Winged Persuasions and veiled Destinies,
Splendours, and Glooms, and glimmering Incarnations
Of hopes and fears, and twilight Phantasies;
And Sorrow, with her family of Sighs,
And Pleasure, blind with tears, led by the gleam
Of her own dying smile instead of eyes,
Came in slow pomp;—the moving pomp might seem
Like pageantry of mist on an autumnal stream.

14

All he had loved, and moulded into thought,
From shape, and hue, and odour, and sweet sound,
Lamented Adonais. Morning sought
Her eastern watchtower, and her hair unbound,
Wet with the tears which should adorn the ground,
Dimmed the aerial eyes that kindle day;
Afar the melancholy thunder moaned,
Pale Ocean in unquiet slumber lay,
And the wild winds flew round, sobbing in their dismay.

15

Lost Echo sits amid the voiceless mountains,
And feeds her grief with his remembered lay,
And will no more reply to winds or fountains,
Or amorous birds perched on the young green spray,
Or herdsman's horn, or bell at closing day;
Since she can mimic not his lips, more dear
Than those for whose disdain she pined away
Into a shadow of all sounds:—a drear
Murmur, between their songs, is all the woodmen hear.

16

Grief made the young Spring wild, and she threw down
Her kindling buds, as if she Autumn were,
Or they dead leaves; since her delight is flown
For whom should she have waked the sullen year?
To Phoebus was not Hyacinth so dear
Nor to himself Narcissus, as to both
Thou Adonais: wan they stand and sere
Amid the faint companions of their youth,
With dew all turned to tears; odour, to sighing ruth.

17

Thy spirit's sister, the lorn nightingale
Mourns not her mate with such melodious pain;
Not so the eagle, who like thee could scale
Heaven, and could nourish in the sun's domain
Her mighty youth with morning, doth complain,
Soaring and screaming round her empty nest,
As Albion wails for thee: the curse of Cain
Light on his head who pierced thy innocent breast,
And scared the angel soul that was its earthly guest!

18

Ah woe is me! Winter is come and gone,
But grief returns with the revolving year;
The airs and streams renew their joyous tone;
The ants, the bees, the swallows reappear;
Fresh leaves and flowers deck the dead Seasons' bier;
The amorous birds now pair in every brake,
And build their mossy homes in field and brere;
And the green lizard, and the golden snake,
Like unimprisoned flames, out of their trance awake.

19

Through wood and stream and field and hill and Ocean
A quickening life from the Earth's heart has burst
As it has ever done, with change and motion,
From the great morning of the world when first
God dawned on Chaos; in its stream immersed
The lamps of Heaven flash with a softer light;
All baser things pant with life's sacred thirst;
Diffuse themselves; and spend in love's delight,
The beauty and the joy of their renewed might.

20

The leprous corpse touched by this spirit tender
Exhales itself in flowers of gentle breath;
Like incarnations of the stars, when splendour
Is changed to fragrance, they illumine death
And mock the merry worm that wakes beneath;
Nought we know, dies. Shall that alone which knows
Be as a sword consumed before the sheath
By sightless lightning?—th' intense atom glows
A moment, then is quenched in a most cold repose.

21

Alas! that all we loved of him should be,
But for our grief, as if it had not been,
And grief itself be mortal! Woe is me!
Whence are we, and why are we? of what scene
The actors or spectators? Great and mean
Meet massed in death, who lends what life must borrow.
As long as skies are blue, and fields are green,
Evening must usher night, night urge the morrow,
Month follow month with woe, and year wake year to sorrow.

22

He will awake no more, oh, never more!
"Wake thou," cried Misery, "childless Mother, rise
Out of thy sleep, and slake, in thy heart's core,
A wound more fierce than his with tears and sighs."
And all the Dreams that watched Urania's eyes,
And all the Echoes whom their sister's song
Had held in holy silence, cried: "Arise!"
Swift as a Thought by the snake Memory stung,
From her ambrosial rest the fading Splendour sprung.

23

She rose like an autumnal Night, that springs
Out of the East, and follows wild and drear
The golden Day, which, on eternal wings,
Even as a ghost abandoning a bier,
Had left the Earth a corpse. Sorrow and fear
So struck, so roused, so rapt Urania;
So saddened round her like an atmosphere
Of stormy mist; so swept her on her way
Even to the mournful place where Adonais lay.

24

Out of her secret Paradise she sped,
Through camps and cities rough with stone, and steel,
And human hearts, which to her aery tread
Yielding not, wounded the invisible
Palms of her tender feet where'er they fell:
And barbed tongues, and thoughts more sharp than they
Rent the soft Form they never could repel,
Whose sacred blood, like the young tears of May,
Paved with eternal flowers that undeserving way.

25

In the death chamber for a moment Death
Shamed by the presence of that living Might
Blushed to annihilation, and the breath
Revisited those lips, and life's pale light
Flashed through those limbs, so late her dear delight.
"Leave me not wild and drear and comfortless,
As silent lightning leaves the starless night!
Leave me not!" cried Urania: her distress
Roused Death: Death rose and smiled, and met her vain caress.

26

"Stay yet awhile! speak to me once again;
Kiss me, so long but as a kiss may live;
And in my heartless breast and burning brain
That word, that kiss shall all thoughts else survive
With food of saddest memory kept alive,
Now thou art dead, as if it were a part
Of thee, my Adonais! I would give
All that I am to be as thou now art!
But I am chained to Time, and cannot thence depart!

27

"Oh gentle child, beautiful as thou wert,
Why didst thou leave the trodden paths of men
Too soon, and with weak hands though mighty heart
Dare the unpastured dragon in his den?
Defenceless as thou wert, oh where was then
Wisdom the mirrored shield, or scorn the spear?
Or hadst thou waited the full cycle, when
Thy spirit should have filled its crescent sphere,
The monsters of life's waste had fled from thee like deer.

28

"The herded wolves, bold only to pursue;
The obscene ravens, clamorous o'er the dead;
The vultures to the conqueror's banner true
Who feed where Desolation first has fed,
And whose wings rain contagion;—how they fled,
When like Apollo, from his golden bow,
The Pythian of the age one arrow sped
And smiled!—The spoilers tempt no second blow,
They fawn on the proud feet that spurn them lying low.

29

"The sun comes forth, and many reptiles spawn;
He sets, and each ephemeral insect then
Is gathered into death without a dawn,
And the immortal stars awake again;
So is it in the world of living men:
A godlike mind soars forth, in its delight
Making earth bare and veiling heaven, and when
It sinks, the swarms that dimmed or shared its light
Leave to its kindred lamps the spirit's awful night."

30

Thus ceased she: and the mountain shepherds came,
Their garlands sere, their magic mantles rent;
The Pilgrim of Eternity, whose fame
Over his living head like Heaven is bent,
An early but enduring monument,
Came, veiling all the lightnings of his song
In sorrow; from her wilds Ierne sent
The sweetest lyrist of her saddest wrong,
And love taught grief to fall like music from his tongue.

31

Midst others of less note, came one frail Form,
A phantom among men; companionless
As the last cloud of an expiring storm
Whose thunder is its knell; he, as I guess,
Had gazed on Nature's naked loveliness,
Actæon-like, and now he fled astray
With feeble steps o'er the world's wilderness,
And his own thoughts, along that rugged way,
Pursued, like raging hounds, their father and their prey.

32

A pardlike Spirit beautiful and swift—
A Love in desolation masked;—a Power
Girt round with weakness;—it can scarce uplift
The weight of the superincumbent hour;
It is a dying lamp, a falling shower,
A breaking billow;—even whilst we speak
Is it not broken? On the withering flower
The killing sun smiles brightly: on a cheek
The life can burn in blood, even while the heart may break.

33

His head was bound with pansies overblown,
And faded violets, white, and pied, and blue;
And a light spear topped with a cypress cone,
Round whose rude shaft dark ivy tresses grew
Yet dripping with the forest's noonday dew,
Vibrated, as the ever-beating heart
Shook the weak hand that grasped it; of that crew
He came the last, neglected and apart;
A herd-abandoned deer struck by the hunter's dart.

34

All stood aloof, and at his partial moan
Smiled through their tears; well knew that gentle band
Who in another's fate now wept his own;
As in the accents of an unknown land,
He sung new sorrow; sad Urania scanned
The Stranger's mien, and murmured: "who art thou?"
He answered not, but with a sudden hand
Made bare his branded and ensanguined brow,
Which was like Cain's or Christ's—Oh! that it should be so!

35

What softer voice is hushed over the dead?
Athwart what brow is that dark mantle thrown?
What form leans sadly o'er the white death-bed,
In mockery of monumental stone,
The heavy heart heaving without a moan?
If it be He, who, gentlest of the wise,
Taught, soothed, loved, honoured the departed one;
Let me not vex, with inharmonious sighs
The silence of that heart's accepted sacrifice.

36

Our Adonais has drunk poison—oh!
What deaf and viperous murderer could crown
Life's early cup with such a draught of woe?
The nameless worm would now itself disown:
It felt, yet could escape the magic tone
Whose prelude held all envy, hate, and wrong,
But what was howling in one breast alone,
Silent with expectation of the song,
Whose master's hand is cold, whose silver lyre unstrung.

37

Live thou, whose infamy is not thy fame!
Live! fear no heavier chastisement from me,
Thou noteless blot on a remembered name!
But be thyself, and know thyself to be!
And ever at thy season be thou free
To spill the venom when thy fangs o'erflow:
Remorse and Self-contempt shall cling to thee;
Hot Shame shall burn upon thy secret brow,
And like a beaten hound tremble thou shalt—as now.

38

Nor let us weep that our delight is fled
Far from these carrion kites that scream below;
He wakes or sleeps with the enduring dead;
Thou canst not soar where he is sitting now.—
Dust to the dust! but the pure spirit shall flow
Back to the burning fountain whence it came,
A portion of the Eternal, which must glow
Through time and change, unquenchably the same,
Whilst thy cold embers choke the sordid hearth of shame.

39

Peace, peace! he is not dead, he doth not sleep—
He hath awakened from the dream of life—
'Tis we, who lost in stormy visions, keep
With phantoms an unprofitable strife,
And in mad trance, strike with our spirit's knife
Invulnerable nothings.—We decay
Like corpses in a charnel; fear and grief
Convulse us and consume us day by day,
And cold hopes swarm like worms within our living clay.

40

He has outsoared the shadow of our night;
Envy and calumny and hate and pain,
And that unrest which men miscall delight,
Can touch him not and torture not again;
From the contagion of the world's slow stain
He is secure, and now can never mourn
A heart grown cold, a head grown grey in vain;
Nor, when the spirit's self has ceased to burn,
With sparkless ashes load an unlamented urn.

41

He lives, he wakes—'tis Death is dead, not he;
Mourn not for Adonais.—Thou young Dawn
Turn all thy dew to splendour, for from thee
The spirit thou lamentest is not gone;
Ye caverns and ye forests, cease to moan!
Cease ye faint flowers and fountains, and thou Air
Which like a mourning veil thy scarf hadst thrown
O'er the abandoned Earth, now leave it bare
Even to the joyous stars which smile on its despair!

42

He is made one with Nature: there is heard
His voice in all her music, from the moan
Of thunder, to the song of night's sweet bird;
He is a presence to be felt and known
In darkness and in light, from herb and stone,
Spreading itself where'er that Power may move
Which has withdrawn his being to its own;
Which wields the world with never wearied love,
Sustains it from beneath, and kindles it above.

43

He is a portion of the loveliness
Which once he made more lovely: he doth bear
His part, while the one Spirit's plastic stress
Sweeps through the dull dense world, compelling there,
All new successions to the forms they wear;
Torturing th' unwilling dross that checks its flight
To its own likeness, as each mass may bear;
And bursting in its beauty and its might
From trees and beasts and men into the Heaven's light.

44

The splendours of the firmament of time
May be eclipsed, but are extinguished not;
Like stars to their appointed height they climb
And death is a low mist which cannot blot
The brightness it may veil. When lofty thought
Lifts a young heart above its mortal lair,
And love and life contend in it, for what
Shall be its earthly doom, the dead live there
And move like winds of light on dark and stormy air.

45

    The inheritors of unfulfilled renown
    Rose from their thrones, built beyond mortal thought,
    Far in the Unapparent, Chatterton
    Rose pale, his solemn agony had not
    Yet faded from him; Sidney, as he fought
    And as he fell and as he lived and loved
    Sublimely mild, a Spirit without spot,
    Arose; and Lucan, by his death approved:
Oblivion as they rose shrank like a thing reproved.

46

    And many more, whose names on Earth are dark
    But whose transmitted effluence cannot die
    So long as fire outlives the parent spark,
    Rose, robed in dazzling immortality.
    "Thou art become as one of us," they cry,
    "It was for thee yon kingless sphere has long
    Swung blind in unascended majesty,
    Silent alone amid an Heaven of song.
Assume thy winged throne, thou Vesper of our throng!"

47

    Who mourns for Adonais? oh come forth
    Fond wretch! and know thyself and him aright.
    Clasp with thy panting soul the pendulous Earth;
    As from a centre, dart thy spirit's light
    Beyond all worlds, until its spacious might
    Satiate the void circumference: then shrink
    Even to a point within our day and night;
    And keep thy heart light lest it make thee sink
When hope has kindled hope, and lured thee to the brink.

48

Or go to Rome, which is the sepulchre
O, not of him, but of our joy: 'tis nought
That ages, empires, and religions there
Lie buried in the ravage they have wrought;
For such as he can lend,—they borrow not
Glory from those who made the world their prey;
And he is gathered to the kings of thought
Who waged contention with their time's decay,
And of the past are all that cannot pass away.

49

Go thou to Rome,—at once the Paradise,
The grave, the city, and the wilderness;
And where its wrecks like shattered mountains rise,
And flowering weeds, and fragrant copses dress
The bones of Desolation's nakedness
Pass, till the Spirit of the spot shall lead
Thy footsteps to a slope of green access
Where, like an infant's smile, over the dead,
A light of laughing flowers along the grass is spread.

50

And grey walls moulder round, on which dull Time
Feeds, like slow fire upon a hoary brand;
And one keen pyramid with wedge sublime,
Pavilioning the dust of him who planned
This refuge for his memory, doth stand
Like flame transformed to marble; and beneath,
A field is spread, on which a newer band
Have pitched in Heaven's smile their camp of death
Welcoming him we lose with scarce extinguished breath.

51

    Here pause: these graves are all too young as yet
    To have outgrown the sorrow which consigned
    Its charge to each; and if the seal is set,
    Here, on one fountain of a mourning mind,
    Break it not thou! too surely shalt thou find
    Thine own well full, if thou returnest home,
    Of tears and gall. From the world's bitter wind
    Seek shelter in the shadow of the tomb.
What Adonais is, why fear we to become?

52

    The One remains, the many change and pass;
    Heaven's light forever shines, Earth's shadows fly;
    Life, like a dome of many-coloured glass,
    Stains the white radiance of Eternity.
    Until Death tramples it to fragments.—Die,
    If thou wouldst be with that which thou dost seek!
    Follow where all is fled!—Rome's azure sky,
    Flowers, ruins, statues, music, words, are weak
The glory they transfuse with fitting truth to speak.

53

    Why linger, why turn back, why shrink, my Heart?
    Thy hopes are gone before; from all things here
    They have departed; thou shouldst now depart!
    A light is past from the revolving year,
    And man, and woman; and what still is dear
    Attracts to crush, repels to make thee wither.
    The soft sky smiles,—the low wind whispers near:
    'Tis Adonais calls! oh, hasten thither,
No more let Life divide what Death can join together.

54

    That Light whose smile kindles the Universe,
    That Beauty in which all things work and move,
    That Benediction which the eclipsing Curse
    Of birth can quench not, that sustaining Love
    Which through the web of being blindly wove
    By man and beast and earth and air and sea,
    Burns bright or dim, as each are mirrors of
    The fire for which all thirst; now beams on me,
Consuming the last clouds of cold mortality.

55

    The breath whose might I have invoked in song
    Descends on me; my spirit's bark is driven,
    Far from the shore, far from the trembling throng
    Whose sails were never to the tempest given;
    The massy earth and sphered skies are riven!
    I am borne darkly, fearfully, afar;
    Whilst burning through the inmost veil of Heaven,
    The soul of Adonais, like a star,
Beacons from the abode where the Eternal are.

2.

"Blood-Hot and Personal":

Mourning Deaths in the Family

"The world is blood-hot and personal," Sylvia Plath commented in "Totem," a meditation on mortality that concludes with a grim vision of flies caught in a spiderweb as "blue children / In nets of the infinite" who have all been "Roped in at the end by the one / Death with its many sticks." But although despite "its many sticks" death *is* in a sense "one"— and an equally sorrowful "one"—for all who suffer it, different deaths are devastating in different ways. Deaths in the family, for instance, have an intimacy that is especially "blood-hot and personal," or so many poems included in this section testify with particular urgency.

Because the family is for most of us the first place or space of being, any change in its configuration can shock or wound. "My mother's life made me a man," asserts John Masefield, wondering what he has "done, or tried, or said / In thanks to that dear woman dead?" At the same time, perhaps because the psychodynamics of family life are so powerful, writers often reiterate them in the moment of mourning. Even after death, writes Adrienne Rich to *her* mother, "You breathe upon us . . . through solid assertions / of yourself." Finally, though, while many poets lament familial losses because they represent—in the words of Elaine Feinstein—the passing of "all that was gentle in / my childhood," some experience such deaths as unnervingly premonitory. With the deaths of grandparents and parents, the ancestral chain that links us to the past sinks into the grave, so such artists realize, as the late William Dickey told his father in an elegiac verse-letter, that soon

> We will come walking toward you,
> seeking you, to kneel clumsily, to lie down,
> to move a little, until the wet earth lets us in.

For, as Dickey adds somberly, "When it needs to, the joining will come"—a "joining" of the quick and the dead that will constitute, he implies, a *re*joining of the "blood-hot and personal" family.

JOHN MASEFIELD

C.L.M.

In the dark womb where I began,
My mother's life made me a man.
Through all the months of human birth
Her beauty fed my common earth.
I cannot see, nor breathe, nor stir,
But through the death of some of her.

Down in the darkness of the grave
She cannot see the life she gave.
For all her love, she cannot tell
Whether I use it ill or well.
Nor knock at dusty doors to find
Her beauty dusty in the mind.

If the grave's gates could be undone,
She would not know her little son,
I am so grown. If we should meet,
She would pass by me in the street,
Unless my soul's face let her see
My sense of what she did for me.

What have I done to keep in mind
My debt to her and womankind?
What woman's happier life repays
Her for those months of wretched days?
For all my mouthless body leeched
Ere Birth's releasing hell was reached?

What have I done, or tried, or said
In thanks to that dear woman dead?

Men triumph over women still,
Men trample women's rights at will,
And man's lust roves the world untamed . . .
O grave, keep shut lest I be shamed.

HUGH MacDIARMID

At My Father's Grave

The sunlicht still on me, you row'd in clood,
We look upon each ither noo like hills
Across a valley. I'm nae mair your son.
It is my mind, nae son o' yours, that looks,
And the great darkness o' your death comes up
And equals it across the way.
A livin' man upon a deid man thinks
And ony sma'er thocht's impossible.

MAY SWENSON

Feel Me

"Feel me to do right," our father said on his deathbed.
We did not quite know—in fact, not at all—what he meant.
His last whisper was spent as through a slot in a wall.
He left us a key, but how did it fit? "Feel me
to do right." Did it mean that, though he died, he would be felt
through some aperture, or by some unseen instrument
our dad just then had come to know? So, to do right always,
we need but feel his spirit? Or was it merely his apology
for dying? "Feel that I do right in not trying,
as you insist, to stay on your side. There is the wide
gateway and the splendid tower, and you implore me
to wait here, with the worms!"

Had he defined his terms, and could we discriminate
among his motives, we might have found out how to "do right"
before *we* died—supposing he felt he suddenly knew
what dying was. "You do wrong because you do not feel
as I do now" was maybe the sense. "Feel me, and emulate
my state, for I am becoming less dense—I am feeling right
for the first time." And then the vessel burst,
and we were kneeling around an emptiness.

We cannot feel our father now. His power courses through us,
yes, but *he*—the chest and cheek, the foot and palm,
the mouth of oracle—is calm. And we still seek
his meaning. "Feel me," he said, and emphasized that word.
Should we have heard it as a plea for a caress—
a constant caress, since flesh to flesh was all that we
could do right if we would bless him?
The dying must feel the pressure of that question—
lying flat, turning cold from brow to heel—the hot

cowards there above protesting their love, and saying,
"What can we do? Are you all right?" While the wall opens
and the blue night pours through. "What can we do?
We want to do what's right."

"Lie down with me, and hold me, tight. Touch me. Be
with me. Feel with me. *Feel* me to do right."

JOHN BERRYMAN

The Marker Slants . . .

from **The Dream Songs** (384)

The marker slants, flowerless, day's almost done,
I stand above my father's grave with rage,
often, often before
I've made this awful pilgrimage to one
who cannot visit me, who tore his page
out: I come back for more,

I spit upon this dreadful banker's grave
who shot his heart out in a Florida dawn
O ho alas alas
When will indifference come, I moan & rave
I'd like to scrabble till I got right down
away down under the grass

and ax the casket open ha to see
just how he's taking it, which he sought so hard
we'll tear apart
the mouldering grave clothes ha & then Henry
will heft the ax once more, his final card,
and fell it on the start.

ROBERT LOWELL

Sailing Home from Rapallo

(February 1954)

Your nurse could only speak Italian,
but after twenty minutes I could imagine your final week,
and tears ran down my cheeks. . . .

When I embarked from Italy with my Mother's body,
the whole shoreline of the *Golfo di Genova*
was breaking into fiery flower.
The crazy yellow and azure sea-sleds
blasting like jack-hammers across
the *spumante*-bubbling wake of our liner,
recalled the clashing colors of my Ford.
Mother travelled first-class in the hold;
her *Risorgimento* black and gold casket
was like Napoleon's at the *Invalides*. . . .

While the passengers were tanning
on the Mediterranean in deck-chairs,
our family cemetery in Dunbarton
lay under the White Mountains
in the sub-zero weather.
The graveyard's soil was changing to stone—
so many of its deaths had been midwinter.
Dour and dark against the blinding snowdrifts,
its black brook and fir trunks were as smooth as masts.
A fence of iron spear-hafts
black-bordered its mostly Colonial grave-slates.

The only "unhistoric" soul to come here
was Father, now buried beneath his recent

unweathered pink-veined slice of marble.
Even the Latin of his Lowell motto:
Occasionem cognosce,
seemed too businesslike and pushing here,
where the burning cold illuminated
the hewn inscriptions of Mother's relatives:
twenty or thirty Winslows and Starks.
Frost had given their names a diamond edge. . . .

In the grandiloquent lettering on Mother's coffin,
Lowell had been misspelled *LOVEL.*
The corpse
was wrapped like *panetone* in Italian tinfoil.

DIANA O'HEHIR

Bedside

Waiting beside my father's bed, watching the pleated sleep, the
      small breathing,
The sheet is so clean and heavy,
It weighs more than my old father does.

My mother has come into the room,
She takes my hand in her young ghost's fingers,
She leans over the bed,
Her dark hair falls in her eyes.

My father's face is bony as a sparrow's body,
His nose pinched like the bird's tight legs, his eyes sculptured
      inside their
Blue eye circles, the forehead
In vine-blue veins.

Here he is now, Mother—
Your bright white husband, your day-warmer, your
World's perfect letter.

She touches a finger to his forehead,
Traces a branching vein
Her hair smells young and dark.

DENISE LEVERTOV

from **The Olga Poems**

I

By the gas-fire, kneeling
to undress,
scorching luxuriously, raking
her nails over olive sides, the red
waistband ring—

(And the little sister
beady-eyed in the bed—
or drowsy, was I? My head
a camera—)

Sixteen. Her breasts
round, round, and
dark-nippled—

who now these two months long
is bones and tatters of flesh in earth.

CAROLYN KIZER

The Great Blue Heron

M.A.K., September, 1880–September, 1955

As I wandered on the beach
I saw the heron standing
Sunk in the tattered wings
He wore as a hunchback's coat.
Shadow without a shadow,
Hung on invisible wires
From the top of a canvas day,
What scissors cut him out?
Superimposed on a poster
Of summer by the strand
Of a long-decayed resort,
Poised in the dusty light
Some fifteen summers ago;
I wondered, an empty child,
"Heron, whose ghost are you?"

I stood on the beach alone,
In the sudden chill of the burned.
My thought raced up the path.
Pursuing it, I ran
To my mother in the house
And led her to the scene.
The spectral bird was gone.

But her quick eye saw him drifting
Over the highest pines
On vast, unmoving wings.
Could they be those ashen things,
So grounded, unwieldy, ragged,

A pair of broken arms
That were not made for flight?
In the middle of my loss
I realized she knew:
My mother knew what he was.

O great blue heron, now
That the summer house has burned
So many rockets ago,
So many smokes and fires
And beach-lights and water-glow
Reflecting pin-wheel and flare:
The old logs hauled away,
The pines and driftwood cleared
From that bare strip of shore
Where dozens of children play;
Now there is only you
Heavy upon my eye.
Why have you followed me here,
Heavy and far away?
You have stood there patiently
For fifteen summers and snows,
Denser than my repose,
Bleaker than any dream,
Waiting upon the day
When, like gray smoke, a vapor
Floating into the sky,
A handful of paper ashes,
My mother would drift away.

ALLEN GINSBERG

from Kaddish

For Naomi Ginsberg 1894–1956

I

Strange now to think of you, gone without corsets & eyes, while
      I walk on the sunny pavement of Greenwich Village.
downtown Manhattan, clear winter noon, and I've been up
      all night, talking, talking, reading the Kaddish aloud,
      listening to Ray Charles blues shout blind on the
      phonograph
the rhythm the rhythm—and your memory in my head three
      years after—And read Adonais' last triumphant stanzas
      aloud—wept, realizing how we suffer—
And how Death is that remedy all singers dream of, sing,
      remember, prophesy as in the Hebrew Anthem, or the
      Buddhist Book of Answers—and my own imagination of
      a withered leaf—at dawn—
Dreaming back thru life, Your time—and mine accelerating
      toward Apocalypse,
the final moment—the flower burning in the Day—and what
      comes after,
looking back on the mind itself that saw an American city
a flash away, and the great dream of Me or China, or you and
      a phantom Russia, or a crumpled bed that never
      existed—
like a poem in the dark—escaped back to Oblivion—
No more to say, and nothing to weep for but the Beings in the
      Dream, trapped in its disappearance,
sighing, screaming with it, buying and selling pieces of phantom,
      worshipping each other,
worshipping the God included in it all—longing or inevitability?—
      while it lasts, a Vision—anything more?

It leaps about me, as I go out and walk the street, look back
    over my shoulder, Seventh Avenue, the battlements of
    window office buildings shouldering each other high,
    under a cloud, tall as the sky an instant—and the sky
    above—an old blue place.
or down the Avenue to the South, to—as I walk toward the
    Lower East Side—where you walked 50 years ago, little
    girl—from Russia, eating the first poisonous tomatoes
    of America—frightened on the dock—
then struggling in the crowds of Orchard Street toward what?—
    toward Newark—
toward candy store, first home-made sodas of the century,
    handchurned ice cream in backroom on musty
    brownfloor boards—
Toward education marriage nervous breakdown, operation,
    teaching school, and learning to be mad, in a dream—
    what is this life?
Toward the Key in the window—and the great Key lays its
    head of light on top of Manhattan, and over the floor,
    and lays down on the sidewalk—in a single vast beam,
    moving, as I walk down First toward the Yiddish
    Theater—and the place of poverty
you knew, and I know, but without caring now—Strange to
    have moved thru Paterson, and the West, and Europe
    and here again,
with the cries of Spaniards now in the doorstoops doors and
    dark boys on the street, fire escapes old as you
—Tho you're not old now, that's left here with me—
Myself, anyhow, maybe as old as the universe—and I guess
    that dies with us—enough to cancel all that comes—
    What came is gone forever every time—
That's good! That leaves it open for no regret—no fear
    radiators, lacklove, torture even toothache in the end—
Though while it comes it is a lion that eats the soul—and the
    lamb, the soul, in us, alas, offering itself in sacrifice to
    change's fierce hunger—hair and teeth—and the roar

of bonepain, skull bare, break rib, rot-skin, braintricked
Implacability.
Ai! ai! we do worse! We are in a fix! And you're out, Death
let you out, Death had the Mercy, you're done with your
century, done with God, done with the path thru it—
Done with yourself at last—Pure—Back to the Babe
dark before your Father, before us all—before the
world—
There, rest. No more suffering for you. I know where you've
gone, it's good.
No more flowers in the summer fields of New York, no joy now,
no more fear of Louis,
and no more of his sweetness and glasses, his high school decades,
debts, loves, frightened telephone calls, conception beds,
relatives, hands—
No more of sister Elanor,—she gone before you—we kept it
secret—you killed her—or she killed herself to bear
with you—an arthritic heart—But Death's killed you
both—No matter—
Nor your memory of your mother, 1915 tears in silent movies
weeks and weeks—forgetting, agrieve watching Marie
Dressler address humanity, Chaplin dance in youth,
or Boris Godinov, Chaliapin's at the Met, halling his voice of a
weeping Czar—by standing room with Elanor & Max
—watching also the Capitalists take seats in Orchestra,
white furs, diamonds,
with the YPSL's hitch-hiking thru Pennsylvania, in black baggy
gym skirts pants, photograph of 4 girls holding each other
round the waste, and laughing eye, too coy, virginal
solitude of 1920
all girls grown old, or dead, now, and that long hair in the
grave—lucky to have husbands later—
You made it—I came too—Eugene my brother before (still
grieving now and will gream on to his last stiff hand, as
he goes thru his cancer—or kill—later perhaps—soon
he will think—)

And it's the last moment I remember, which I see them all,
    thru myself, now—tho not you
I didn't foresee what you felt—what more hideous gape of
    bad mouth came first—to you—and were you prepared?
To go where? In that Dark—that—in that God? a radiance?
    A Lord in the Void? Like an eye in the black cloud in a
    dream? Adonoi at last, with you?
Beyond my remembrance! Incapable to guess! Not merely the
    yellow skull in the grave, or a box of worm dust, and
    a stained ribbon—Deathshead with Halo? can you
    believe it?
Is it only the sun that shines once for the mind, only the flash
    of existence, than none ever was?
Nothing beyond what we have—what you had—that so pitiful
    —yet Triumph,
to have been here, and changed, like a tree, broken, or flower—
    fed to the ground—but mad, with its petals, colored,
    thinking Great Universe, shaken, cut in the head, leaf
    stript, hid in an egg crate hospital, cloth wrapped, sore
    —freaked in the moon brain, Naughtless.
No flower like that flower, which knew itself in the garden, and
    fought the knife—lost
Cut down by an idiot Snowman's icy—even in the Spring—
    strange ghost thought—some Death—Sharp icicle in
    his hand—crowned with old roses—a dog for his eyes
    —cock of a sweatshop—heart of electric irons.
All the accumulations of life, that wear us out—clocks, bodies,
    consciousness, shoe, breasts—begotten sons—your Com-
    munism—'Paranoia' into hospitals.
You once kicked Elanor in the leg, she died of heart failure
    later. You of stroke. Asleep? within a year, the two of
    you, sisters in death. Is Elanor happy?
Max grieves alive in an office on Lower Broadway, lone large
    mustache over midnight Accountings, not sure. His life
    passes—as he sees—and what does he doubt now?
    Still dream of making money, or that might have made

money, hired nurse, had children, found even your
    Immortality, Naomi?
I'll see him soon. Now I've got to cut through—to talk to you
    —as I didn't when you had a mouth.
Forever. And we're bound for that, Forever—like Emily
    Dickinson's horses—headed to the End.
They know the way—These Steeds—run faster than we think
    —it's our own life they cross—and take with them.

      Magnificent, mourned no more, marred of heart, mind behind, married dreamed, mortal changed—Ass and face done with murder.

      In the world, given, flower maddened, made no Utopia, shut under pine, almed in Earth, balmed in Lone, Jehovah, accept.

      Nameless, One Faced, Forever beyond me, beginningless, endless, Father in death. Tho I am not there for this Prophecy, I am unmarried, I'm hymnless, I'm Heavenless, headless in blisshood I would still adore

      Thee, Heaven, after Death, only One blessed in Nothingness, not light or darkness, Dayless Eternity—

      Take this, this Psalm, from me, burst from my hand in a day, some of my Time, now given to Nothing—to praise Thee—But Death

      This is the end, the redemption from Wilderness, way for the Wonderer, House sought for All, black handkerchief washed clean by weeping—page beyond Psalm—Last change of mine and Naomi—to God's perfect Darkness—Death, stay thy phantoms!

WILLIAM DICKEY

The Shortest Day

To the Memory of Ralph Dickey

The white room that I eat in and write in
is filled with the wet light of a winter afternoon.
It is the shortest day.

Tangerines, lemons,
bright yellow candles in bright lacquer holders.
I use these to hold on with. To try.

You yourself have taken your darkness away with you
and somewhere in this wet enormous country now
you are lying, as thin as you could ever have wished to be.

It is a little harder, here, without you.
The light lessens, and the voices of shouting children
distance themselves in the ending of this cold year.

Be at some ease. We will come walking toward you,
seeking you, to kneel clumsily, to lie down,
to move a little, until the wet earth lets us in.

Now, for you, I am lighting a candle, and another,
So as to kill myself not this night, but another.
But that is only time. When it needs to, the joining will come.

I wish I could ask you to wait for me
there where you are in the night, at least touch my hand,
at least say to me, "Quiet, now. Come in."

ADRIENNE RICH

A Woman Mourned by Daughters

Now, not a tear begun,
we sit here in your kitchen,
spent, you see, already.
You are swollen till you strain
this house and the whole sky.
You, whom we so often
succeeded in ignoring!
You are puffed up in death
like a corpse pulled from the sea;
we groan beneath your weight.
And yet you were a leaf,
a straw blown on the bed,
you had long since become
crisp as a dead insect.
What is it, if not you,
that settles on us now
like satin you pulled down
over our bridal heads?
What rises in our throats
like food you prodded in?
Nothing could be enough.
You breathe upon us now
through solid assertions
of yourself: teaspoons, goblets,
seas of carpet, a forest
of old plants to be watered,
an old man in an adjoining
room to be touched and fed.
And all this universe
dares us to lay a finger
anywhere, save exactly
as you would wish it done.

ELAINE FEINSTEIN

Dad

Your old hat hurts me, and those black
    fat raisins you liked to press into
my palm from your soft heavy hand.
    I see you staggering back up the path
with sacks of potatoes from some local farm,
    fresh eggs, flowers. Every day I grieve

for your great heart broken and you gone.
    You loved to watch the trees. This year
you did not see their Spring.
    The sky was freezing over the fen
as on that somewhere secretly appointed day
    you beached: cold, white-faced, shivering.

What happened, old bull, my loyal
    hoarse-voiced warrior? The hammer
blow that stopped you in your track
    and brought you to a hospital monitor
could not destroy your courage
    to the end you were
uncowed and unconcerned with pleasing anyone.

I think of you now as once again safely
    at my mother's side, the earth as
chosen as a bed, and feel most sorrow for
    all that was gentle in
my childhood buried there
    already forfeit, now forever lost.

TONY HARRISON

Flood

His home address was inked inside his cap
and on every piece of paper that he carried
even across the church porch of the snap
that showed him with mi mam just minutes married.

But if ah'm found at 'ome (he meant found dead)
turn t'water off. Through his last years he nursed,
more than a fear of dying, a deep dread
of his last bath running over, or a burst.

Each night towards the end he'd pull the flush
then wash, then in pyjamas, rain or snow,
go outside, kneel down in the yard, and push
the stopcock as far off as it would go.

For though hoping that he'd drop off in his sleep
he was most afraid, I think, of not being 'found'
there in their house, his ark, on firm Leeds ground
but somewhere that kept moving, cold, dark, deep.

SEAMUS HEANEY

from **Clearances** (Sonnets 2, 3, 7)

2

Polished linoleum shone there. Brass taps shone.
The china cups were very white and big—
An unchipped set with sugar bowl and jug.
The kettle whistled. Sandwich and teascone
Were present and correct. In case it run,
The butter must be kept out of the sun.
And don't be dropping crumbs. Don't tilt your chair.
Don't reach. Don't point. Don't make noise when you stir.

It is Number 5, New Row, Land of the Dead,
Where grandfather is rising from his place
With spectacles pushed back on a clean bald head
To welcome a bewildered homing daughter
Before she even knocks. 'What's this? What's this?'
And they sit down in the shining room together.

3

When all the others were away at Mass
I was all hers as we peeled potatoes.
They broke the silence, let fall one by one
Like solder weeping off the soldering iron:
Cold comforts set between us, things to share
Gleaming in a bucket of clean water.
And again let fall. Little pleasant splashes
From each other's work would bring us to our senses.

So while the parish priest at her bedside
Went hammer and tongs at the prayers for the dying
And some were responding and some crying

I remembered her head bent towards my head,
Her breath in mine, our fluent dipping knives—
Never closer the whole rest of our lives.

7

In the last minutes he said more to her
Almost than in all their life together.
'You'll be in New Row on Monday night
And I'll come up for you and you'll be glad
When I walk in the door . . . Isn't that right?'
His head was bent down to her propped-up head.
She could not hear but we were overjoyed.
He called her good and girl. Then she was dead,
The searching for a pulsebeat was abandoned
And we all knew one thing by being there.
The space we stood around had been emptied
Into us to keep, it penetrated
Clearances that suddenly stood open.
High cries were felled and a pure change happened.

RICHARD GARCIA

Mi Mamá, the Playgirl

When my mother left Mexico, soldiers commandeered the train, forcing the passengers to get off and wait for the next one. Later they passed it lying on its side, burning.

She wore black dresses. Her closet was lined with identical pairs of black shoes. She constantly advised me to jump off the bridge while the tide was going out.

Long after my father was dead, she complained that his side of the bed still sank down. "*Viejo*," she would tell him, "If you have somewhere to go, please go." At seventy, she went out to nightclubs. Twisted her knee doing the bunny hop. Talked for hours to forty-year-old lovers on the phone. My brothers were ashamed.

After she died, she came to see me as she had promised. My father came, too. We sat around in the kitchen drinking coffee as if nothing had happened. My father looked great, said he'd been working out. She stroked his forearm, smiling at his tattoo of the dancing hula girl. When they left it was nothing dramatic. They just walked out the door and up a street that seemed to reach into the night sky. How beautiful, I thought, as I was waking, the stars shining in my mother's hair.

MARILYN HACKER

Autumn 1980

for Judith McDaniel

I spent the night after my mother died
in a farmhouse north of Saratoga Springs
belonging to a thirty-nine-year-old
professor with long, silvered wiry hair,
a lively girl's flushed cheeks and gemstone eyes.
I didn't know that she had died.
Two big bitches and a varying
heap of cats snoozed near a black woodstove
on a rag rug, while, on the spring-shot couch,
we talked late over slow glasses of wine.
In the spare room near Saratoga Springs
was a high box bed. My mother died
that morning, of heart failure, finally.
Insulin shocks burned out her memory.
On the bed, a blue early-century
Texas Star, in a room white and blue
as my flannel pajamas. I'd have worn
the same, but smaller, ten years old at home.
Home was the Bronx, on Eastburn Avenue,
miles south of the hermetic not-quite-new
block where they'd sent this morning's ambulance.
Her nurse had telephoned. My coat was on,
my book-stuffed bag already on my back.
She said, "Your mother had another shock.
We'll be taking her to the hospital."
I asked if I should stay. She said, "It's all
right." I named the upstate college where
I'd speak that night. This had happened before.
I knew / I didn't know: it's not the same.

November cold was in that corner room
upstairs, with a frame window over land
the woman and another woman owned
—who was away. I thought of her alone
in her wide old bed, me in mine. I turned
the covers back. I didn't know she had died.
The tan dog chased cats; she had to be tied
in the front yard while I went along
on morning errands until, back in town,
I'd catch my bus. November hills were raw
fall after celebratory fall
foliage, reunions, festival.
I blew warmth on my hands in a dark barn
where two shaggy mares whuffled in straw,
dipped steaming velvet muzzles to the pail
of feed. We'd left the pickup's heater on.
It smelled like kapok when we climbed inside.
We both unzipped our parkas for the ride
back to the Saratoga bus station.
I blamed the wind if I felt something wrong.
A shrunken-souled old woman whom I saw
once a month lay on a hospital
slab in the Bronx. Mean or not, that soul
in its cortege of history was gone.
I didn't know that I could never know,
now, the daughtering magic to recall
across two coffee mugs the clever Young
Socialist whose views would coincide
with mine. I didn't know that she had died.
Not talking much, while weighted sky pressed down,
we climbed the back road's bosom to the all-
night diner doubling as a bus depot.
I brushed my new friend's cool cheek with my own,
and caught the southbound bus from Montreal.
I counted boarded-up racetrack motel
after motel. I couldn't read. I tried

to sleep. I didn't know that she had died.
Hours later, outside Port Authority,
rained on, I zipped and hooded an obscure
ache from my right temple down my shoulder.
Anonymous in the midafternoon
crowds, I'd walk, to stretch, I thought, downtown.
I rode on the female wave, typically
into Macy's (where forty-five years
past, qualified by her new M.A.
in Chemistry, she'd sold Fine Lingerie),
to browse in Fall Sale bargains for my child,
aged six, size eight, hung brilliantly or piled
like autumn foliage I'd missed somehow,
and knew what I officially didn't know
and put the bright thing down, scalded with tears.

WENDY BARKER

Trying To

As if under this wood a spirit could rise.
Rubbing and rubbing, I am unable to leave
the smoothness of tables, the cool
surface of kitchen counters. Fingerprints
on the bathroom mirrors I wipe away.
As if everything in this house
could gleam with its own right shape.

There are things that happen everyone says
could not be helped, there was nothing
anyone could do. I am trying to believe that.
I try not to say every morning when the line
of trees sharpens the bedroom window: If only.
If only I would have, he might have.

We have now had the dividing of spoils.
He would have said it like that, with a grin.
My son keeps his last four rolls
of Stick-O-Pep lifesavers, says he will
keep them unopened in memory of Grandfather,
maybe once a year peel back the foil
and suck just one, for good luck.
The brothers-in-law own more ties
than they ever thought they wanted.
Last month we sorted the books, shipped
boxes to each of the sisters.

When I rub and rub, the refrigerator
glows like a white shrine.
The sun folds clean stripes across the bed,
the sheets lie flat, unrumpled.

The bed sits squarely in the room.
This morning I had not wanted to leave it.
I sleep with his travel alarm
by my head, his silver bookmark
digging its delicate arrow
into the meat of my book.

JAMES TATE

The Lost Pilot

for my father, 1922–1944

Your face did not rot
like the others—the co-pilot,
for example, I saw him

yesterday. His face is corn-
mush: his wife and daughter,
the poor ignorant people, stare

as if he will compose soon.
He was more wronged than Job.
But your face did not rot

like the others—it grew dark,
and hard like ebony;
the features progressed in their

distinction. If I could cajole
you to come back for an evening,
down from your compulsive

orbiting, I would touch you,
read your face as Dallas,
your hoodlum gunner, now,

with the blistered eyes, reads
his braille editions. I would
touch your face as a disinterested

scholar touches an original page.
However frightening, I would
discover you, and I would not

turn you in; I would not make
you face your wife, or Dallas,
or the co-pilot, Jim. You

could return to your crazy
orbiting, and I would not try
to fully understand what

it means to you. All I know
is this: when I see you,
as I have seen you at least

once every year of my life,
spin across the wilds of the sky
like a tiny, African god,

I feel dead. I feel as if I were
the residue of a stranger's life,
that I should pursue you.

My head cocked toward the sky,
I cannot get off the ground.
and, you, passing over again,

fast, perfect, and unwilling
to tell me that you are doing
well, or that it was mistake

that placed you in that world,
and me in this: or that misfortune
placed these worlds in us.

ALAN WILLIAMSON

Arrangements

Choosing the coffin,
unfinished redwood,
            searching
the plasterboard record-stores of Monterey
for the one music, Erik
Satie's *Trois Gymnopédies,*
            telling
the distinguished guests to stay away;
               leaving my father,

where he taught me to know
a landscape not to the heart's liking,
no image of its peace, but cypress
tightened to the shape of wind
              but you loved it, singing
"My little gray home in the West," as you pulled down the driveway.

.   .   .

In the year of the Crash, when Hart Crane
fought his parents for the strength of an instant's writing,
you gave half your salary to yours,
gave up your poetry,
and waited (fifteen years)
            to have a child.

But set out gaily to be death on feeling
unfused with intellect
           off to gay/gray London,
you and Mama schemed to give each other
a first edition of Lord Rochester,

long watched, with anxious pricing, in its window
                                    shadowed by the British Museum.
Were your twenties lighter-spirited than mine?

In your essay I at last sit reading,
you three years dead,
you argue that John Donne
"may not have violated his own integrity"
if, on "plumbing the emotional depth of that
inconstancy" that first so pleased him

> *So flowes her face, and thine eyes, neither now*
> *That Saint, nor Pilgrime*

—an invisible darkening, a moon eclipsed, reason's pale taper
more windblown—
                                    he turned to the single Light.

After one operation, you went back
to Camp-Meeting terrors: Hell
a great ring of heat pressing you down,
                                    afraid
it might graze the hems of those who stood by
robed in mysterious coolness.

But you died the modern way, knowing
the strength of your disease, but not its name,
with no preachers or Bibles, but your peculiar God,
and the tiny bright-horned marble bull I brought you
from Crete, I don't know why . . .
                                    You angered Mama
by your habit of only sleeping sideways,
your hand closed on the bed's steel guard-rail;
you apologized, saying
"I've spent so many nights in hospitals
I began to feel it was friendly."

And later, open-armed
for the last cardiogram,
ringed with wife, son, an outer sphere of nurses,
you said, "My faithful people,"
your eyes dark violets
like a farm boy's the first
time he thinks a girl likes him.

GREGORY ORR

Gathering the Bones Together

For Peter Orr
(1951–1959)

When all the rooms of the house
fill with smoke, it's not enough
to say an angel is sleeping on the chimney.

1. A NIGHT IN THE BARN

The deer carcass hangs from a rafter.
Wrapped in blankets, a boy keeps watch
from a pile of loose hay. Then he sleeps

and dreams about a death that is coming:
Inside him, there are small bones
scattered in a field
among burdocks and dead grass.
He will spend his life walking there,
gathering the bones together.

Pigeons rustle in the eaves.
At his feet, the German shepherd
snaps its jaws in its sleep.

2.

A father and his four sons
run down a slope toward
a deer they just killed.
The father and two sons carry
rifles. They laugh, jostle,

and chatter together.
A gun goes off,
and the youngest brother
falls to the ground.
A boy with a rifle
stands beside him, screaming.

3.

I crouch in the corner of my room,
staring into the glass well
of my hands; far down
I see him drowning in air.

Outside, leaves shaped like mouths
make a black pool
under a tree. Snails glide
there, little death-swans.

4. SMOKE

Something has covered the chimney
and the whole house fills with smoke.
I go outside and look up at the roof,
but I can't see anything.
I go back inside. Everyone weeps,
walking from room to room.
Their eyes ache. This smoke
turns people into shadows.
Even after it is gone,
and the tears are gone,
we will smell it in pillows
when we lie down to sleep.

5.

He lives in a house of black glass.
Sometimes I visit him and we talk.
My father says he is dead,
but what does that mean?

Last night I found a child
sleeping on a nest of bones.
He had a red, leaf-shaped
scar on his cheek. I lifted him up
and carried him with me, though
I didn't know where I was going.

6. THE JOURNEY

Each night, I knelt on a marble slab
and scrubbed at the blood.
I scrubbed for years and still it was there.

But tonight the bones in my feet
begin to burn. I stand up
and start walking, and the slab
appears under my feet with each step,
a white road only as long as your body.

7. THE DISTANCE

The winter I was eight, a horse
slipped on the ice, breaking its leg.
Father took a rifle, a can of gasoline.
I stood by the road at dusk and watched
the carcass burning in the far pasture.

I was twelve when I killed him;
I felt my own bones wrench from my body.
Now I am twenty-seven and walk
beside this river, looking for them.
They have become a bridge
that arches toward the other shore.

YUSEF KOMUNYAKAA

from Songs for My Father

I told my brothers I heard
You & mother making love,
Your low moans like a blues
Bringing them into the world.
I didn't know if you were laughing
Or crying. I held each one down
& whispered your song in their ears.
Sometimes I think they're still jealous
Of our closeness, having forgotten
We had to square-off & face each other,
My fists balled & cocked by haymakers.
That spring I lifted as many crossties
As you. They can't believe I can
Remember when you had a boy's voice.

           .   .   .

Goddamn you. Goddamn you.
If you hit her again, I'll sail through
That house like a dustdevil.
Everyone & everything here
Is turning against you,
That's why I had to tie the dog
To a tree before you could chastise us.
He darted like lightning through the screen door.
I know you'll try to kill me
When it happens. You know
I'm your son & it's bound to happen.
Sometimes I close my eyes till I am
On a sea of falling dogwood blossoms,
But someday this won't work.

           .   .   .

I never said thanks for Butch,
The wooden dog you pulled by a string.
It was ugly as a baldheaded doll.
Patched with wire & carpenter's glue, something
I didn't believe you had ever loved.
I am sorry for breaking it in half.
I never meant to make you go
Stand under the falling snowflakes
With your head bowed on Christmas
Day. I couldn't look at Butch
& see that your grandmother Julia,
The old slave woman who beat you
As if that's all she knew, had put love
Into it when she carved the dog from oak.

.   .   .

You spoke with your eyes
Last time I saw you, cramped
Between a new wife & the wall. You couldn't
Recognize funeral dirt stamped down
With dancesteps. Your name & features half
X-ed out. I could see your sex,
Your shame, a gold-toothed pout,
As you made plans for the next house you'd build,
Determined to prove me wrong. I never knew
We looked so much like each other. Before
I could say I loved you, you began talking money,
Teasing your will with a cure in Mexico.
You were skinny, bony, but strong enough to try
Swaggering through that celestial door.

JILL BIALOSKY

After father died

from Fathers in the Snow

2.

After father died
the love was all through the house
untamed and sometimes violent.
When the dates came we went up to our rooms
and mother entertained.
Frank Sinatra's "Strangers in the Night,"
the smell of Chanel No. 5 in her hair and the laughter.
We sat crouched at the top of the stairs.
In the morning we found mother asleep on the couch
her hair messed, and the smell
of stale liquor in the room.
We knelt on the floor before her,
one by one touched our fingers
over the red flush in her face.
The chipped sunlight through the shutters.
It was a dark continent
we and mother shared;
it was sweet and lonesome,
the wake men left in our house.

LI-YOUNG LEE

This Hour and What Is Dead

Tonight my brother, in heavy boots, is walking
through bare rooms over my head,
opening and closing doors.
What could he be looking for in an empty house?
What could he possibly need there in heaven?
Does he remember his earth, his birthplace set to torches?
His love for me feels like spilled water
running back to its vessel.

At this hour, what is dead is restless
and what is living is burning.

Someone tell him he should sleep now.

My father keeps a light on by our bed
and readies for our journey.
He mends ten holes in the knees
of five pairs of boy's pants.
His love for me is like his sewing:
various colors and too much thread,
the stitching uneven. But the needle pierces
clean through with each stroke of his hand.

At this hour, what is dead is worried
and what is living is fugitive.

Someone tell him he should sleep now.

God, that old furnace, keeps talking
with his mouth of teeth,
a beard stained at feasts, and his breath

of gasoline, airplane, human ash.
His love for me feels like fire,
feels like doves, feels like river-water.

At this hour, what is dead is helpless, kind
and helpless. While the Lord lives.

Someone tell the Lord to leave me alone.
I've had enough of his love
that feels like burning and flight and running away.

FRANCISCO ARAGON

Tricycles

to my mother (1932–1997)

Metal-gray, sturdy—
those heavy-duty ones we rode
on Fridays: being led
out of a bright church
basement and through swinging
glass doors into that dim
seemingly round room—hardwood
floor we circled counter
clockwise pedaling and
pedaling with exuberant deter-
mination, as if to play
were a serious matter, which
it was: me and a friend climbing
off, leaving them riderless,

sneaking up spiral stairs, exploring
the pews, organ chamber, statue
of what looked like—I never told you—
a lipsticked Virgin, the chemical
smell of synthetic carpet

—burned, torn down two terms
after we "graduated": the empty lot
we'd pass heading for Cala
Foods (you'd let me push
the cart)—for years wild with weeds
till it became the space
it is today, *The Palm Broker*
selling trees on Guerrero St.

—it's now

I know
the shield you were those frugal years . . .

And the long-haired man
who sat in the sandbox
with us on warm days—once,
after it fell from my hands, I ate
a crunchy noisy sandwich;
I thought he was a Beatle, driving
you mad: *Revolution* screeching
over and over on Maria's
turntable at home a block away

And the black and white
photograph snapped of me
I glimpsed in a manila envelope
the other day—the moving
picture in my head
sharpening into focus

of you

in that basement
crouching at a low table:
those geometric shapes
like stained glass only plastic
the click and snap of attaching
them to each other—helping me
for ten, fifteen minutes
before whispering
in my ear, disappearing behind

the door I rise towards when I grow
tired of waiting . . . What is it
exactly, I'm feeling
when I see you're gone, that brings
wetness to my cheeks, wetness

absent decades later before
your casket? What was it
I began to lose
that first day? How well
you knew me then, knowing
that tricking me
                    was how
that first morning
you'd get me to stay.

3.

"How You Call to Me, Call to Me":

Lamenting the Death of the Beloved

"Exactly half the phenomenal world is gone," writes Paul Monette as he laments the loss of his lover in "Half Life." And half a life is precisely what those who mourn a dead beloved feel they have been left. "See what you miss by being dead?" Ruth Stone sardonically asks her long-gone husband in "Curtains," while Donald Hall tells his dead wife that "Your presence in this house / is almost as enormous / and painful as your absence."

For all who mourn dead spouses, lovers, partners, the world seems to have been split apart, with massive absence replacing what had been passionate presence. Even apparently trivial details of daily life are transformed by such an experience, as many attest. It's "hard for me to cook my meals / From recipes she used," confesses Douglas Dunn, as he outlines the grief he feels in each "kitchen pilgrimage," and Tess Gallagher comically admits to consuming her dead husband's favorite foods—"last of his Wheat Chex, last / of his 5-Quick-Cinnamon-Rolls-With-Icing"— while "Chanting: he'd-want-me- / to-he'd-want-me-to." But, she adds tellingly, "something eats with me, a darling of / the air-that-is,": the absent presence of the beloved for whom all these poets yearn.

To many elegists, indeed, this absent presence, this "darling of / the air-that-is," becomes so vivid, so plausible and nearly "real" that it metamorphoses into a seductive yet ghostly figure, luring, beckoning. "Woman much missed, how you call to me, call to me," exclaims Thomas Hardy in an address to his dead wife. And for others, the nearness, the virtual immanence of such a figure is radically disorienting. As she broods on memories of her husband in a railway station ("I remember you running beside the train waving good-bye"), Ruth Stone wonders "Am I going toward you or away from you on this train?" In the minds of those for whom "exactly half the phenomenal world is gone," past and future all too often blur into a bewildering mist.

JOHN MILTON

Methought I Saw My Late Espousèd Saint

Methought I saw my late espousèd saint
  Brought to me like Alcestis from the grave,
  Whom Jove's great son to her glad husband gave,
  Rescued from death by force though pale and faint.
Mine, as whom washed from spot of childbed taint,
  Purification in the old law did save,
  And such, as yet once more I trust to have
  Full sight of her in heaven without restraint,
Came vested all in white, pure as her mind.
  Her face was veiled, yet to my fancied sight
  Love, sweetness, goodness, in her person shined
So clear, as in no face with more delight.
  But O, as to embrace me she inclined,
  I waked, she fled, and day brought back my night.

LADY CATHERINE DYER

My Dearest Dust

Epitaph on monument erected in 1641 by Lady Catherine Dyer to her
husband Sir William Dyer in Colmworth Church, Bedfordshire

My dearest dust, could not thy hasty day
Afford they drowzy patience leave to stay
One hower longer: so that we might either
Sate up, or gone to bedd together?
But since thy finisht labor hath possest
Thy weary limbs with early rest,
Enjoy it sweetly: and thy widdowe bride
Shall soone repose her by thy slumbering side.
Whose business, now, is only to prepare
My nightly dress, and call to prayre:
Mine eyes wax heavy and ye day growes old.
The dew falls thick, my beloved growes cold.
Draw, draw ye closed curtaynes: and make room:
My dear, my dearest dust; I come, I come.

WILLIAM WORDSWORTH

She Dwelt Among the Untrodden Ways

She dwelt among the untrodden ways
    Beside the springs of Dove,
A Maid whom there were none to praise
    And very few to love:

A violet by a mossy stone
    Half hidden from the eye!
—Fair as a star, when only one
    Is shining in the sky.

She lived unknown, and few could know
    When Lucy ceased to be;
But she is in her grave, and, oh,
    The difference to me!

WILLIAM WORDSWORTH

A Slumber Did My Spirit Seal

A slumber did my spirit seal;
   I had no human fears:
She seemed a thing that could not feel
   The touch of earthly years.

No motion has she now, no force;
   She neither hears nor sees;
Rolled round in earth's diurnal course,
   With rocks, and stones, and trees.

EMILY BRONTË

R. Alcona to J. Brenzaida

Cold in the earth, and the deep snow piled above thee!
Far, far removed, cold in the dreary grave!
Have I forgot, my Only Love, to love thee,
Severed at last by Time's all-wearing wave?

Now, when alone, do my thoughts no longer hover
Over the mountains on Angora's shore;
Resting their wings where heath and fern-leaves cover
That noble heart for ever, ever more?

Cold in the earth, and fifteen wild Decembers
From those brown hills have melted into spring—
Faithful indeed is the spirit that remembers
After such years of change and suffering!

Sweet Love of youth, forgive if I forget thee
While the World's tide is bearing me along:
Sterner desires and darker hopes beset me,
Hopes which obscure but cannot do thee wrong.

No other Sun has lightened up my heaven;
No other Star has ever shone for me:
All my life's bliss from thy dear life was given—
All my life's bliss is in the grave with thee.

But when the days of golden dreams had perished
And even Despair was powerless to destroy,
Then did I learn how existence could be cherished,
Strengthened and fed without the aid of joy;

Then did I check the tears of useless passion,
Weaned my young soul from yearning after thine;
Sternly denied its burning wish to hasten
Down to that tomb already more than mine!

And even yet, I dare not let it languish,
Dare not indulge in Memory's rapturous pain;
Once drinking deep of that divinest anguish,
How could I seek the empty world again?

THOMAS HARDY

The Going

Why did you give no hint that night
That quickly after the morrow's dawn,
And calmly, as if indifferent quite,
You would close your term here, up and be gone
      Where I could not follow
      With wing of swallow
To gain one glimpse of you ever anon!

      Never to bid good-bye,
      Or lip me the softest call,
Or utter a wish for a word, while I
Saw morning harden upon the wall,
      Unmoved, unknowing
      That your great going
Had place that moment, and altered all.

Why do you make me leave the house
And think for a breath it is you I see
At the end of the alley of bending boughs
Where so often at dusk you used to be;
      Till in darkening dankness
      The yawning blankness
Of the perspective sickens me!

      You were she who abode
      By those red-veined rocks far West,
You were the swan-necked one who rode
Along the beetling Beeny Crest,
      And, reining nigh me,
      Would muse and eye me,
While Life unrolled us its very best.

Why, then, latterly did we not speak,
Did we not think of those days long dead,
And ere your vanishing strive to seek
That time's renewal? We might have said,
    'In this bright spring weather
    We'll visit together
Those places that once we visited.'

    Well, well! All's past amend,
    Unchangeable. It must go.
I seem but a dead man held on end
To sink down soon. . . . O you could not know
    That such swift fleeing
    No soul foreseeing—
Not even I—would undo me so!

THOMAS HARDY

The Voice

Woman much missed, how you call to me, call to me,
Saying that now you are not as you were
When you had changed from the one who was all to me,
But as at first, when our day was fair.

Can it be you that I hear? Let me view you, then,
Standing as when I drew near to the town
Where you would wait for me: yes, as I knew you then,
Even to the original air-blue gown!

Or is it only the breeze, in its listlessness
Travelling across the wet mead to me here,
You being ever dissolved to wan wistlessness,
Heard no more again far or near?

    Thus I; faltering forward,
    Leaves around me falling,
Wind oozing thin through the thorn from norward,
    And the woman calling.

RUTH STONE

Winter

The ten o'clock train to New York,
coaches like loaves of bread powdered with snow.
Steam wheezes between the couplings.
Stripped to plywood, the station's cement standing room
imitates a Russian novel. It is now that I remember you.
Your profile becomes the carved handle of a letter knife.
Your heavy-lidded eyes slip under the seal of my widowhood.
It is another raw winter. Stray cats are suffering.
Starlings crowd the edges of chimneys.
It is a drab misery that urges me to remember you.
I think about the subjugation of women and horses;
brutal exposure; weather that forces, that strips.
In our time we met in ornate stations
arching up with nineteenth-century optimism.
I remember you running beside the train waving good-bye.
I can produce a facsimile of you standing
behind a column of polished oak to surprise me.
Am I going toward you or away from you on this train?
Discarded junk of other minds is strewn beside the tracks:
mounds of rusting wire, grotesque pop art of dead motors,
senile warehouses. The train passes a station;
fresh people standing on the platform,
their faces expecting something.
I feel their entire histories ravish me.

RUTH STONE

Curtains

Putting up new curtains,
other windows intrude.
As though it is that first winter in Cambridge
when you and I had just moved in.
Now cold borscht alone in a bare kitchen.

What does it mean if I say this years later?

Listen, last night
I am on a crying jag
with my landlord, Mr. Tempesta.
I sneaked in two cats.
He screams NO PETS! NO PETS!
I become my Aunt Virginia,
proud but weak in the head.
I remember Anna Magnani.
I throw a few books. I shout.
He wipes his eyes and opens his hands.
OK OK keep the dirty animals
but no nails in the walls.
We cry together.
I am so nervous, he says.

I want to dig you up and say, look,
it's like the time, remember,
when I ran into our living room naked
to get rid of that fire inspector.

See what you miss by being dead?

JUDITH WRIGHT

"Rosina Alcona to Julius Brenzaida"

Living long is containing
archaean levels,
buried yet living.
Greek urns, their lovely tranquillity
still and yet moving,
directing, surviving.

So driving homewards
full of my present
along the new freeway,
carved straight, rushing forward.
I see suddenly there still
that anachronism, the old wooden pub
stranded at the crossways.

Where you and I once
in an absolute present
drank laughing
in a day still living,
still laughing, still permanent.

Present crossed past
synchronized, at the junction.
The daylight of one day
was deepened, was darkened
by the light of another.

Three faces met,
your vivid face in life,
your face of dead marble
touched mine simultaneously.

Holding the steering-wheel
my hands freeze. Out of my eyes
jump these undryable tears
from artesian pressures,
from the strata that cover you,
the silt-sift of time.

These gulping dry lines
are not my song for you.
That's made already.
Come in, dead Emily.

Have I forgot, my only Love, to love thee.
Severed at last by time's all-wearing wave?

A work of divinest anguish,
a Greek urn completed:
I grip the steering-wheel.
No other star has ever shone for me.

The pure poem rises
in lovely tranquillity,
as the Greek urn rises
from the soil of the past,
as the lost face rises
and the tears return.

I move through my present
gripping the steering-wheel,
repeating, repeating it.
The crossways fade; the freeway rushes forward.
"These days obscure but cannot do thee wrong."

PETER DAVISON

Under the Roof of Memory

(In Memory of Jane Davison)

1. PLEAS

Please help us keep your memory alive.
When I leaf through what's left of you, stacked up
into a formless pile of crumbling paper,
my hand turns pages, and occasions blur
until I stoop for a mishandled pill
and cannot straighten up. Or yawn. Then
a whiff of the heat lightning of desire
flickers at the fragrance of a caress
forty years old, a darkened room in Kansas.
Who shall deliver me from the body of this death?

2. CELEBRATION

You floated weightlessly above your body,
in utterances aerating anything
that crept within your reach. You loved releasing
the preposterous, always managing to fold it
into a phrase, as when you located *Star Wars*
as taking place in "the Marseilles of the galaxy."
Dwindling through the waning days of life,
you wrote in your last letter, "Simplify,
simplify seems to be the method to deal
with the uncertainties of my health, as we
apply rational faculties to solve problems
we never really thought of as problems: who
carries the dirty laundry down to the machine
in the basement, and who carries it up,"
Setting your house in order. Simplifying it
into a church as your body prepared to die.

3. REMONSTRANCE

Why can't you take your rest? You have been dead
so long that every cell of you has entered
my helplessly surviving body, leaching down
beneath the landscape to our children,
to the dear actuality of my second wife.
You could, like her first husband, live with us
as an invisible, cherished, and welcome presence.
You would be past sixty now. You would have stiffened,
whitened, would feel aches of your own,
and shuffle, smiling at your own decline
and other such absurdities: my own.

4. CRITIQUE

Is it worth much, this sedulous retelling
of the careworn beads of the body? Why must I
catalogue its youthful urges, its middle-aged
infelicities, its eldering need to finger
its entrances, dark witnesses to history?
Get shut of the obsessive self-regard
of the child, that temperature chart more passionate
in the terms of description than in the thing described!
What price forgetfulness? What price peace?

5. ENVOI

Late in my life, I dream of us together,
clothed in the house whose peaked, protective roof
floats without burden over spacious rooms,
commodious, airy, bright as a church. Its walls
and roof, pulled out of touch by the intervention of time,
hold up a screen for love, a sleight of words.
We longed to keep a ravenous world at bay
by gazing down its glare and speaking well.

DONALD HALL

Letter with No Address

Your daffodils rose up
and collapsed in their yellow
bodies on the hillside
garden above the bricks
you laid out in sand, squatting
with pants pegged and face
masked like a beekeeper's
against the black flies.
Buttercups circle the planks
of the old wellhead
this May while your silken
gardener's body withers or moulds
in the Proctor graveyard.
I drive and talk to you crying
and come back to this house
to talk to your photographs.

There's news to tell you:
Maggie Fisher's pregnant.
I carried myself like an egg
at Abigail's birthday party
a week after you died,
as three-year-olds bounced
uproarious on a mattress.
Joyce and I met for lunch
at the mall and strolled weepily
through Sears and B. Dalton.

Today it's four weeks
since you lay on our painted bed

and I closed your eyes.
Yesterday I cut irises to set
in a pitcher on your grave;
today I brought a carafe
to fill it with fresh water.
I remember bone pain,
vomiting, and delirium. I remember
pond afternoons.

           My routine
is established: coffee;
the *Globe*; breakfast;
writing you this letter
at my desk. When I go to bed
to sleep after baseball,
Gus follows me into the bedroom
as he used to follow us.
Most of the time he flops
down in the parlor
with his head on his paws.

Once a week I drive to Tilton
to see Dick and Nan.
Nan doesn't understand much
but she knows you're dead;
I feel her fretting. The tune
of Dick and me talking
seems to console her.

           You know now
whether the soul survives death.
Or you don't. When you were dying
you said you didn't fear
punishment. We never dared
to speak of Paradise.

At five A.M., when I walk outside,
mist lies thick on hayfields.
By eight the air is clear,
cool, sunny with the pale yellow
light of mid-May. Kearsarge
rises huge and distinct,
each birch and balsam visible.
To the west the waters
of Eagle Pond waver
and flash through popples just
leafing out.

               Always the weather,
writing its book of the world,
returns you to me.
Ordinary days were best,
when we worked over poems
in our separate rooms.
I remember watching you gaze
out the January window
into the garden of snow
and ice, your face rapt
as you imagined burgundy lilies.

Your presence in this house
is almost as enormous
and painful as your absence.
Driving home from Tilton,
I remember how you cherished
that vista with its center
the red door of a farmhouse
against green fields.

Are you past pity?
If you have consciousness now,

if something I can call
"you" has something
like "consciousness," I doubt
you remember the last days.
I play them over and over:
I lift your wasted body
onto the commode, your arms
looped around my neck, aiming
your bony bottom so that
it will not bruise on a rail.
Faintly you repeat,
"Momma, Momma."

        You lay
astonishing in the long box
while Alice Ling prayed
and sang "Amazing Grace"
a cappella. Three times today
I drove to your grave.
Sometimes, coming back home
to our circular driveway,
I imagine you've returned
before me, bags of groceries upright
in the back of the Saab,
its trunk lid delicately raised
as if proposing an encounter,
dog-fashion, with the Honda.

SANDRA M. GILBERT

June 15, 1992: Widow's Walk, Harpswell, Maine

A moon like a bloody animal eye over the inlet,
low, low toward the hill as if struggling
to cool itself in the chill black salt of the mudflats;
and the salt stench of the marshes simmers around
the tipsy wharf I walk on.

             My dear,
I ate what I was told to try—
tonight chowder, lobster, sweet corn
and a blueberry muffin; last night clams
and lobster, steamed, baked, stewed.

Yesterday Joanne and I wandered through Bath,
admiring the white and black whalers' mansions,
the widow's walks where stoic wives
paced with straining eyes, scanning the long
flat sea for specks of motion.

And I sucked in the light flung out by the sea
at Popham Beach, drank up the buckets of salt wind
shifting the pale New England sands.
I'm stuffed with this state where we summered
thirty years ago.

          Remember
the cabin on Frenchman's Bay,
swelled with our secret heat, under the covers,
while bats flapped through the pines
and moths banged on the screens?

That's how I feel:
                        bloated with love
too heavy to hold, fat as the past.
The wharf rocks with the weight
of what I carry—

                        myself and you,
too much for one scared woman,
yet I'm looking for more,
pacing and looking,
as if any minute now,

in the lingering blue of almost solstice,
the old tour boat might sputter up to me,
me and you at the rails,
squinting against the sun
and eager for souvenirs.

DOUGLAS DUNN

Dining

No more in supermarkets will her good taste choose
  Her favourite cheese and lovely things to eat,
Or, hands in murmuring tubs, sigh as her fingers muse
  Over the mundane butter, mundane meat.
Nor round the market stalls of France will Lesley stroll
  Appraising aubergines, *langoustes, patisseries*
And artichokes, or hear the poultry vendors call,
  Watch merchants slicing spokes in wheels of Brie.
My lady loved to cook and dine, but never more
  Across starched linen and the saucy pork
Can we look forward to *Confit de Périgord.*
  How well my lady used her knife and fork!
Happy together—ah, my lady loved to sport
  And love. She loved the good; she loved to laugh
And loved so many things, infallible in art
  That pleased her, water, oil or lithograph,
With her own talent to compose the world in light.
  And it is hard for me to cook my meals
From recipes she used, without that old delight
  Returning, masked in sadness, until it feels
As if I have become a woman hidden in me—
  Familiar with each kitchen-spotted page,
Each stain, each note in her neat hand a sight to spin me
  Into this grief, this kitchen pilgrimage.
O my young wife, how sad I was, yet pleased, to see
  And help you eat the soup that Jenny made
On your last night, who all that day had called for tea,
  And only that, or slept your unafraid,
Serene, courageous sleeps, then woke, and asked for tea—
  "Nothing to eat. Tea. Please"—lucid and polite.
Eunice, Daphne, Cresten, Sandra, how you helped me,

To feed my girl and keep her kitchen bright.
Know that I shake with gratitude, as, Jenny, when
    My Lesley ate your soup on her last night,
That image of her as she savoured rice and lemon
    Refused all grief, but was alight
    With nature, courage, friendship, appetite.

TESS GALLAGHER

Crazy Menu

Last of his toothpaste, last of his Wheat Chex, last
of his 5-Quick-Cinnamon-Rolls-With-Icing, his
Pop Secret Microwave Pop-
corn, his Deluxe Fudge Brownie Mix next to my
Casbah Nutted Pilaf on the sparser
shelf, I'm using it all up. Chanting: he'd-want-me-
to-he'd-want-me-to. To consume loss like a hydra-headed
meal of would-have-dones accompanied by
missed-shared-delight. What can I tell you?
I'm a lost proof.
But something eats with me, a darling of
the air-that-is. It smacks its unkissable lips and
pours me down with a gleam in its unblinkable eye, me —
the genius loci of his waiting room to this feast of rapidly
congealing unobtainables. Oh-me-of-
the-last-of-his-lastness through which I am gigantically
left over like the delight of Turkish

Delight. Don't haul out your memory vault to
cauterize my green-with-moment-thumb. Or shove me
into the gloom-closet of yet another cannibalistic
Nevermore. I've been there. And there too. It was not
unusual — that bravado of a castrato in a brothel
yanking his nose and waxing paradisal. No, I'm more like
a Polish miner who meets a Chinese miner at a
helmet convention in Amsterdam. Because we both
speak a brand of Philip Morris English picked up
from a now extinct murmur heard only impromptu
at a certain caved-in depth, we are overwhelmed by
the sheer fact of meeting and we clasp
each other by our bare heads for nights, exchanging

the unimpoverishable secrets of the earth, the going down and
the coming up, the immutable pretext of light, a common history
of slumped canaries, of bereaved kinfolk, of black-lunged
singers and handmade coffins. We trade
a few eulogies and drinking songs and sit down at last to
a huge meal of aged cheese and kippers.
We lean into our vitals

with all the lights off. It's dark inside and out.
This is our last chance to revel in the unencumbered
flickering of Balinese tapers we bought at
a souvenir stand above the canal. Like rice and spit
we are tolerant of all occasions, this being
the lifting of the dread whereby
the girls' wings we autograph onto our duffle coats
have been painted like butterflies, only
on the upside so the dark is mocked by
our raised arms, our fluttered concentration, uncollectable as
the lastness I am of him I love-ed
scribbled unsentimentally on a valentine in 1983:
       To the King of my Heart!
In daylight we pick up our tinned rations and hike off,
every artery and nerve of us, into the rest
of our commemorative lives.

PAUL MONETTE

Half Life

exactly half the phenomenal world is gone
look you can see it take anything *anything*
roses a half corona of petals red lush
half black rot now the aching mountains Heidi
on the east slope west face strip-mined singed
as if by lava houses up and down the street
half pink stucco curtains breezing the windows
half smithereens dead toys melted lawn chairs
in my case I think it's the left side closest
to you in bed I get up and half of me doesn't
work I drag me like a broken wing my good
eye sees flesh and green the dead eye an X-
ray gaping at skeletons I could bear it
if the fugue went back and forth but the skull's
the bedrock truth just as I'm the friendless
kid who never made it out of Andover MA
and all the while you are getting more whole Rog
even as the world is cleaved in two I open
the door to the morning and half the city's
Capri and half Buchenwald how is it you
so vanished so cut down such proof of the end
of all gentle men how is it you spring full-blown
from a thousand fragments it's like picking up
a shard of red-black vase off a Greek hillside
looks like part of a sandal and a girl's long hair
in a flash the white-stone city rises entire
around you full of just men who live to be
90 the buried pieces fit I blow up pictures
to 5 by 7 and stare in your eyes and you're
all there more finely boned more grown than I
and always looking at me the cavorting dunce

of the Nikon wild as a tourist with ten minutes
left in Rome life's mostly snapshots oh how
I want the rest of me to be the rest of you
but cut in half like this how can I I read
your '80 diary its limpid accounts the blessed
dailiness gold as winter sunset and you say
Paul had a bad meeting or *Paul's upset*
about NOTHING I SWEAR IT WAS NOTHING AT ALL
I was totally intact and didn't know and
now the sun's cold as the moon and rivers
die mid-cataract the species from N to
Z are extinct not a tiger left leafing
two months through '80 clucking at your mood
swings I practically forget it's like you're
going to walk in and compass the world again
and the west face of everything will torrent
with orchids and streams of honey a Bengal
roaring from the escarpment Rog I am not
reconciled not a millimeter unless
you count the dead-fish fin that was my hand
the stump of my running foot this side
of me that's halfway there see I must've loved
life too much in our time doubtless this is
to balance me out so I live in what's left of
the evidence not out there in the rotting
garden the firebombed street and Plato's myth
of lovers the fated meeting of equal halves
is a tale for lonely kids there's no act III
the sundering with its howl that never ends
waits till the pictures are shot to sever east
and west like a man bound spreadeagle to four
horses bolting for the corners of an earth
half ash half mad nothing what it was mine
the skull in the field and once I had it all

4.

"Sorrow's Springs":

Grieving for the Deaths of Children

"Here lies resting, out of breath, / Out of turns, Elizabeth" begins X. J. Kennedy's poignant elegy "for a child who skipped rope." And as this poet implies, the deaths of children have always seemed especially cruel precisely because, like this little girl who is "out of [her] turns" at the game of jump rope, such deaths have happened out of turn—out of the normal or ordinary sequencing of the generations, in which the young ought by rights, in their turn at life, to outlive the old. Nor can the child yet understand the death that may threaten her too soon. In "Spring and Fall," a delicate meditation addressed "to a young child" (though not *about* a child), Gerard Manley Hopkins tries to explain that "Sorrow's springs are the same," whether one grieves for the fall of leaves, for "Goldengrove unleaving" in the autumn, or for the loss of life, "the blight man was born for." Yet surely no parent confronted with the death of a beloved son or daughter would approach the loss quite so philosophically, nor could a child encompass it so neatly. Rather, as Paula Meehan writes in her powerful and passionate "Child Burial," if she suspected her baby would meet an untimely death, many a mother "would spin / time back" and even "cancel the love feast / the hot night of your making."

BEN JONSON

On My First Son

Farewell, thou child of my right hand, and joy;
My sin was too much hope of thee, loved boy:
Seven years thou wert lent to me, and I thee pay,
Exacted by thy fate, on the just day.
O could I lose all father now! For why
Will man lament the state he should envy,
To have so soon 'scaped world's and flesh's rage,
And, if no other misery, yet age?
Rest in soft peace, and asked, say, "Here doth lie.
Ben Jonson his best piece of poetry."
For whose sake henceforth all his vows be such
As what he loves may never like too much.

ANNE BRADSTREET

In Memory of My Dear Grandchild Anne Bradstreet, Who Deceased June 20, 1669, Being Three Years and Seven Months Old

With troubled heart and trembling hand I write,
The heavens have changed to sorrow my delight.
How oft with disappointment have I met,
When I on fading things my hopes have set.
Experience might 'fore this have made me wise,
To value things according to their price.
Was ever stable joy yet found below?
Or perfect bliss without mixture of woe?
I knew she was but as a withering flower,
That's here today, perhaps gone in an hour;
Like as a bubble, or the brittle glass,
Or like a shadow turning as it was.
More fool then I to look on that was lent
As if mine own, when thus impermanent.
Farewell dear child, thou ne'er shall come to me,
But yet a while, and I shall go to thee;
Meantime my throbbing heart's cheered up with this:
Thou with thy Savior art in endless bliss.

KATHERINE PHILIPS

On the Death of My First and Dearest Child, Hector Philips, Borne the 23d of April, and Died the 2d of May 1655

Twice forty months in wedlock I did stay.
    Then had my vows crowned with a lovely boy.
And yet in forty days he dropped away:
    O! swift vicissitude of human joy!

I did but see him, and he disappeared.
    I did but touch the rosebud, and it fell;
A sorrow unforeseen and scarcely feared.
    So ill can mortals their afflictions spell.

And now (sweet babe) what can my trembling heart
    Suggest to right my doleful fate or thee?
Tears are my muse, and sorrow all my art.
    So piercing groans must be thy elegy.

Thus whilst no eye is witness of my moan,
    I grieve thy loss (Ah, boy too dear to live!)
And let the unconcernèd world alone.
    Who neither will, nor can, refreshment give.

An offering too for thy sad tomb I have,
    Too just a tribute to thy early hearse;
Receive these gasping numbers to thy grave.
    The last of thy unhappy mother's verse.

CHRISTINA ROSSETTI

Why did baby die . . . ?

Why did baby die,
Making Father sigh,
Mother cry?

Flowers, that bloom to die,
Make no reply
Of 'why?'
But bow and die.

ALICE MEYNELL

Maternity

One wept whose only child was dead,
  New-born, ten years ago.
'Weep not; he is in bliss,' they said.
  She answered, 'Even so,

'Ten years ago was born in pain
  A child, not now forlorn.
But oh, ten years ago, in vain,
  A mother, a mother was born.'

ELIZABETH BISHOP

First Death in Nova Scotia

In the cold, cold parlor
my mother laid out Arthur
beneath the chromographs:
Edward, Prince of Wales,
with Princess Alexandra,
and King George with Queen Mary.
Below them on the table
stood a stuffed loon
shot and stuffed by Uncle
Arthur, Arthur's father.

Since Uncle Arthur fired
a bullet into him,
he hadn't said a word.
He kept his own counsel
on his white, frozen lake,
the marble-topped table.
His breast was deep and white,
cold and caressable;
his eyes were red glass,
much to be desired.

"Come," said my mother,
"Come and say good-bye
to your little cousin Arthur."
I was lifted up and given
one lily of the valley
to put in Arthur's hand.
Arthur's coffin was
a little frosted cake,
and the red-eyed loon eyed it
from his white, frozen lake.

Arthur was very small.
He was all white, like a doll
that hadn't been painted yet.
Jack Frost had started to paint him
the way he always painted
the Maple Leaf (Forever).
He had just begun on his hair,
a few red strokes, and then
Jack Frost had dropped the brush
and left him white, forever.

The gracious royal couples
were warm in red and ermine;
their feet were well wrapped up
in the ladies' ermine trains.
They invited Arthur to be
the smallest page at court.
But how could Arthur go,
clutching his tiny lily,
with his eyes shut up so tight
and the roads deep in snow?

WILLIAM STAFFORD

For a Lost Child

What happens is, the kind of snow that sweeps
Wyoming comes down while I'm asleep. Dawn
finds our sleeping bag but you are gone.
Nowhere now, you call through every storm,
a voice that wanders without a home.

Across bridges that used to find a shore
you pass, and along shadows of trees that fell
before you were born. You are a memory
too strong to leave this world that slips away
even as its precious time goes on.

I glimpse you often, faithful to every country
we ever found, a bright shadow the sun
forgot one day. On a map of Spain
I find your note left from a trip that year
our family traveled: "Daddy, we could meet here."

X. J. KENNEDY

Little Elegy

for a child who skipped rope

Here lies resting, out of breath,
Out of turns, Elizabeth
Whose quicksilver toes not quite
Cleared the whirring edge of night.

Earth whose circles round us skim
Till they catch the lightest limb,
Shelter now Elizabeth
And for her sake trip up Death.

LUCILLE CLIFTON

the lost baby poem

the time i dropped your almost body down
down to meet the waters under the city
and run one with the sewage to the sea
what did i know about waters rushing back
what did i know about drowning
or being drowned

you would have been born into winter
in the year of the disconnected gas
and no car   we would have made the thin
walk over Genesee hill into the Canada wind
to watch you slip like ice into strangers' hands
you would have fallen naked as snow into winter

if you were here i could tell you these
and some other things

if i am ever less than a mountain
for your definite brothers and sisters
let the rivers pour over my head
let the sea take me for a spiller
of seas   let black men call me stranger
always   for your never named sake

MARILYN NELSON

I Decide Not to Have Children

Dawn, the gulls weep for the Jews,
and up through my muddy blood
my lost sister rises like a drowned puppy.
I'd forgotten how far away
I'd sent her, wonder how it was
in that wet country,
her skin melting back into mine.
There were nights
I almost recognized her face,
like an old rose pressed under glass.
Sometimes she made
a knock in the pipes
faint as a heartbeat
and backed away again.

In some small room of myself
she has shrunk
to the size of a sparrow
since the night the soldiers came
and searched through my dreams
in their angry uniforms.
I find her there, halfway to sleep,
a sister smaller than a hare
in the blind appendix
behind my eyes.

I'd forgotten how much I cared
and she comes holding out

her fat brown fists,
the flowers of mourning
already twisted in her hair.
Her faint body made a light
that warmed the whole house.

PAULA MEEHAN

Child Burial

Your coffin looked unreal,
fancy as a wedding cake.

I chose your grave clothes with care,
your favourite stripey shirt,

your blue cotton trousers.
They smelt of woodsmoke, of October,

your own smell there too.
I chose a gansy of handspun wool,

warm and fleecy for you. It is
so cold down in the dark.

No light can reach you and teach you
the paths of wild birds,

the names of the flowers,
the fishes, the creatures.

Ignorant you must remain
of the sun and its work,

my lamb, my calf, my eaglet,
my cub, my kid, my nestling,

my suckling, my colt. I would spin
time back, take you again

within my womb, your amniotic lair,
and further spin you back

through nine waxing months
to the split seeding moment

you chose to be made flesh,
word within me.

I'd cancel the love feast
the hot night of your making.

I would travel alone
to a quiet mossy place,

you would spill from me into the earth
drop by bright red drop.

5.

"How Far from then Forethought of ":

Mourning the Deaths of Friends

The deaths of friends are often mirrors for our own unknowable deaths, or for death itself. "Lycidas" and "Adonais," those two paradigms of elegy, were addressed to lost friends, as was Tennyson's great and influential sequence *In Memoriam*, one of the most popular works in Victorian England. In all these texts, the deaths of friends force mourning poets to confront the meaning of mortality, the inscrutability of fate, and the nature of nature itself. Often, too, however, the deaths of friends remind the poet who records them of the changing shape his or her own individual life has taken. "With rue my heart is laden," confides A. E. Housman, "For golden friends I had," and nearly a century later Derek Walcott echoes that lament, with its implicit prayer for the past to be revived, restored:

> Half my friends are dead.
> I will make you new ones, said earth.
> No, give them back, as they were, instead,
> with faults and all, I cried.

To have the past and one's friends of the past back, however, is not just to have beloved people back "faults and all" but also to regain innocence. For as Gerard Manley Hopkins writes in his moving lament for "Felix Randal the farrier" (the blacksmith), death was not "forethought"—was "far from then forethought of"—in the pride of health and youth, the "boisterous years," that first brought many loving comrades together.

THOMAS GRAY

Sonnet on the Death of Richard West

In vain to me the smiling mornings shine.
   And reddening Phoebus lifts his golden fire;
The birds in vain their amorous descant join,
   Or cheerful fields resume their green attire;
These ears, alas! for other notes repine,
   A different object do these eyes require;
My lonely anguish melts no heart but mine,
   And in my breast the imperfect joys expire.
Yet morning smiles the busy race to cheer,
   And newborn pleasure brings to happier men;
The fields to all their wonted tribute bear;
   To warm their little loves the birds complain:
I fruitless mourn to him that cannot hear,
   And weep the more, because I weep in vain.

ALFRED, LORD TENNYSON

from In Memoriam

7

Dark house, by which once more I stand
  Here in the long unlovely street,
  Doors, where my heart was used to beat
So quickly, waiting for a hand,

A hand that can be clasped no more—
  Behold me, for I cannot sleep,
  And like a guilty thing I creep
At earliest morning to the door.

He is not here; but far away
  The noise of life begins again,
  And ghastly through the drizzling rain
On the bald street breaks the blank day.

8

A happy lover who has come
  To look on her that loves him well,
  Who 'lights and rings the gateway bell,
And learns her gone and far from home;

He saddens, all the magic light
  Dies off at once from bower and hall,
  And all the place is dark, and all
The chambers emptied of delight:

So find I every pleasant spot
  In which we two were wont to meet,
  The field, the chamber, and the street,
For all is dark where thou art not.

Yet as that other, wandering there
    In those deserted walks, may find
    A flower beat with rain and wind,
Which once she fostered up with care;

So seems it in my deep regret,
    O my forsaken heart, with thee
    And this poor flower of poesy
Which little cared for fades not yet.

But since it pleased a vanished eye,
    I go to plant it on his tomb,
    That if it can it there may bloom,
Or dying, there at least may die.

67

When on my bed the moonlight falls,
    I know that in thy place of rest
    By that broad water of the west
There comes a glory on the walls:

Thy marble bright in dark appears,
  · As slowly steals a silver flame
    Along the letters of thy name,
And o'er the number of thy years.

The mystic glory swims away,
    From off my bed the moonlight dies;
    And closing eaves of wearied eyes
I sleep till dusk is dipped in gray;

And then I know the mist is drawn
    A lucid veil from coast to coast,
    And in the dark church like a ghost
Thy tablet glimmers to the dawn.

CHRISTINA ROSSETTI

My Friend

Two days ago with dancing glancing hair,
    With living lips and eyes:
    Now pale, dumb, blind, she lies;
So pale, yet still so fair.

We have not left her yet, not yet alone;
    But soon must leave her where
    She will not miss our care,
Bone of our bone.

Weep not; O friends, we should not weep:
    Our friend of friends lies full of rest;
    No sorrow rankles in her breast,
Fallen fast asleep.

She sleeps below,
    She wakes and laughs above:
    Today, as she walked, let us walk in love;
Tomorrow follow so.

GERARD MANLEY HOPKINS

Felix Randal

Felix Randal the farrier, O is he dead then? my duty all ended,
Who have watched his mould of man, big-boned and hardy-handsome
Pining, pining, till time when reason rambled in it and some
Fatal four disorders, fleshed there, all contended?

Sickness broke him. Impatient, he cursed at first, but mended
Being anointed and all; though a heavenlier heart began some
Months earlier, since I had our sweet reprieve and ransom
Tendered to him. Ah well, God rest him all road ever he offended!

This seeing the sick endears them to us, us too it endears.
My tongue had taught thee comfort, touch had quenched thy tears,
Thy tears that touched my heart, child, Felix, poor Felix Randal;

How far from then forethought of, all thy more boisterous years,
When thou at the random grim forge, powerful amidst peers,
Didst fettle for the great grey drayhorse his bright and battering sandal!

A. E. HOUSMAN

With Rue My Heart Is Laden

With rue my heart is laden
  For golden friends I had,
For many a rose-lipt maiden
  And many a lightfoot lad.

By brooks too broad for leaping
  The lightfoot boys are laid;
The rose-lipt girls are sleeping
  In fields where roses fade.

EDNA ST. VINCENT MILLAY

from **Memorial to D.C.**

V

ELEGY

Let them bury your big eyes
In the secret earth securely,
Your thin fingers, and your fair,
Soft, indefinite-coloured hair,—
All of these in some way, surely,
From the secret earth shall rise;
Not for these I sit and stare,
Broken and bereft completely:
Your young flesh that sat so neatly
On your little bones will sweetly
Blossom in the air.

But your voice . . . never the rushing
Of a river underground,
Not the rising of the wind
In the trees before the rain,
Not the woodcock's watery call,
Not the note the white-throat utters,
Not the feet of children pushing
Yellow leaves along the gutters
In the blue and bitter fall,
Shall content my musing mind
For the beauty of that sound
That in no new way at all
Ever will be heard again.

Sweetly through the sappy stalk
Of the vigourous weed,

Holding all it held before,
Cherished by the faithful sun,
On and on eternally
Shall your altered fluid run,
Bud and bloom and go to seed:
But your singing days are done;
But the music of your talk
Never shall the chemistry
Of the secret earth restore.
All your lovely words are spoken.
Once the ivory box is broken,
Beats the golden bird no more.

THEODORE ROETHKE

Elegy for Jane

My Student, Thrown by a Horse

I remember the neckcurls, limp and damp as tendrils;
And her quick look, a sidelong pickerel smile;
And how, once startled into talk, the light syllables leaped for her,
And she balanced in the delight of her thought,
A wren, happy, tail into the wind,
Her song trembling the twigs and small branches.
The shade sang with her;
The leaves, their whispers turned to kissing;
And the mold sang in the bleached valleys under the rose.

Oh, when she was sad, she cast herself down into such a pure depth,
Even a father could not find her:
Scraping her cheek against straw;
Stirring the clearest water.

My sparrow, you are not here,
Waiting like a fern, making a spiny shadow.
The sides of wet stones cannot console me,
Nor the moss, wound with the last light.

If only I could nudge you from this sleep,
My maimed darling, my skittery pigeon.
Over this damp grave I speak the words of my love:
I, with no rights in this matter,
Neither father nor lover.

JANE COOPER

Long, Disconsolate Lines

in memory of Shirley Eliason Haupt

Because it is a gray day but not snowy, because traffic grinds by outside,
because I woke myself crying *help!* to no other in my bed and no god,
because I am in confusion about god,
because the tree out there with its gray, bare limbs is shaped like a lyre,
but it is only January, nothing plays it, no lacerating March sleet,
no thrum of returning rain,
because its arms are empty of buds or even of protective snow,
I am in confusion, words harbor in my throat, I hear not one confident
     tune,
and however long I draw out this sentence
it will not arrive at any truth.

It's true my friend died in September and I have not yet begun to mourn.
Overnight, without warning, the good adversary knocked at her door,
the one she so often portrayed
as a cloud-filled drop out the cave's mouth, crumpled dark of an old
     garden chair. . . .
But a lyre-shaped tree? yes, a lyre-shaped tree. It's true that at twenty-four
in the dripping, raw Iowa woods
she sketched just such a tree, and I saw it, fell in love with its half-
     heard lament
as if my friend, in her pristine skin, already thrashed by the storm-
     blows ahead,
had folded herself around them,
as if she gave up nothing, as if she sang.

GARY SNYDER

For John Chappell

Over the Arafura sea, the China sea,
    Coral sea, Pacific
chains of volcanoes in the dark—
you in Sydney where it's summer;
I imagine that last ride outward
late at night.
                stiff new gears—tight new engine
up some highway I have never seen
too fast—too fast—
    like I said at Tango
        when you went down twice on gravel—

Did you have a chance to think
o shit I've fucked it now
instant crash and flight and sudden death—
    Malaya, Indonesia
    Taiwan, the Philippines, Okinawa
        families sleeping—reaching—
        humans by the millions
        world of breathing flesh,

me in Kyoto. You in Australia
wasted in the night.
black beard, mad laugh, and sadly serious brow.
    earth lover; shaper and maker.
        potter, cooker,

    now be clay in the ground.

DEREK WALCOTT

Sea Canes

Half my friends are dead.
I will make you new ones, said earth.
No, give me them back, as they were, instead,
with faults and all, I cried.

Tonight I can snatch their talk
from the faint surf's drone
through the canes, but I cannot walk

on the moonlit leaves of ocean
down that white road alone,
or float with the dreaming motion

of owls leaving earth's load.
O earth, the number of friends you keep
exceeds those left to be loved.

The sea canes by the cliff flash green and silver;
they were the seraph lances of my faith,
but out of what is lost grows something stronger

that has the rational radiance of stone,
enduring moonlight, further than despair,
strong as the wind, that through dividing canes

brings those we love before us, as they were,
with faults and all, not nobler, just there.

LINDA PASTAN

Death's Blue-Eyed Girl

When did the garden with its banked flowers
start to smell like a funeral chapel,
and the mild breeze passing our foreheads
to feel like the back of a nurse's hand
testing for fever? We used to be
immortal in our ignorance, sending
our kites up for the lightning, swimming
in unknown waters at night and naked.
Death was a kind of safety net to catch us
if we fell too far. Remember Elaine
standing in April, a child on one hip
for ballast, her head distracted with poems?
The magician waved and bowed, showed us his
empty sleeves and she was gone.

ROBERT PINSKY

Impossible to Tell

To Robert Hass and in memory of Elliot Gilbert

Slow dulcimer, gavotte and bow, in autumn,
Bashō and his friends go out to view the moon;
In summer, gasoline rainbow in the gutter,

The secret courtesy that courses like ichor
Through the old form of the rude, full-scale joke,
Impossible to tell in writing. *"Bashō"*

He named himself, "Banana Tree": banana
After the plant some grateful students gave him,
Maybe in appreciation of his guidance

Threading a long night through the rules and channels
Of their collaborative linking-poem
Scored in their teacher's heart: live, rigid, fluid

Like passages etched in a microscopic circuit.
Elliot had in his memory so many jokes
They seemed to breed like microbes in a culture

Inside his brain, one so much making another
It was impossible to tell them all:
In the court-culture of jokes, a top banana.

Imagine a court of one: the queen a young mother,
Unhappy, alone all day with her firstborn child
And her new baby in a squalid apartment

Of too few rooms, a different race from her neighbors.
She tells the child she's going to kill herself.
She broods, she rages. Hoping to distract her,

The child cuts capers, he sings, he does imitations
Of different people in the building, he jokes,
He feels if he keeps her alive until the father

Gets home from work, they'll be okay till morning.
It's laughter *versus* the bedroom and the pills.
What is he in his efforts but a courtier?

Impossible to tell his whole delusion.
In the first months when I had moved back East
From California and had to leave a message

On Bob's machine, I used to make a habit
Of telling the tape a joke; and part-way through,
I would pretend that I forgot the punchline.

Or make believe that I was interrupted —
As though he'd be so eager to hear the end
He'd have to call me back. The joke was Elliot's,

More often than not. The doctors made the blunder
That killed him some time later that same year.
One day when I got home I found a message

On my machine from Bob. He had a story
About two rabbis, one of them tall, one short,
One day while walking along the street together

They see the corpse of a Chinese man before them,
And Bob said, sorry, he forgot the rest.
Of course he thought that his joke was a dummy.

Impossible to tell—a dead-end challenge
But here it is, as Elliot told it to me:
The dead man's widow came to the rabbis weeping,

Begging them, if they could, to resurrect him.
Shocked, the tall rabbi said absolutely not.
But the short rabbi told her to bring the body

Into the study house, and ordered the shutters
Closed so the room was night-dark. Then he prayed
Over the body, chanting a secret blessing

Out of Kabala. "Arise and breathe," he shouted;
But nothing happened. The body lay still. So then
The little rabbi called for hundreds of candles

And danced around the body, chanting and praying
In Hebrew, then Yiddish, then Aramaic. He prayed
In Turkish and Egyptian and Old Galician

For nearly three hours, leaping about the coffin
In the candlelight so that his tiny black shoes
Seemed not to touch the floor. With one last prayer

Sobbed in the Spanish of before the Inquisition
He stopped, exhausted, and looked in the dead man's face.
Panting, he raised both arms in a mystic gesture

And said, "Arise and breathe!" And still the body
Lay as before. Impossible to tell
In words how Elliot's eyebrows flailed and snorted

Like shaggy mammoths as—the Chinese widow
Granting permission—the little rabbi sang
The blessing for performing a circumcision

And removed the dead man's foreskin, chanting blessings
In Finnish and Swahili, and bathed the corpse
From head to foot, and with a final prayer

In Babylonian, gasping with exhaustion,
He seized the dead man's head and kissed the lips
And dropped it again and leaping back commanded,

"Arise and breathe!" The corpse lay still as ever.
At this, as when Bashō's disciples wind
Along the curving spine that links the *renga*

Across the different voices, each one adding
A transformation according to the rules
Of stasis and repetition, all in order

And yet impossible to tell beforehand,
Elliot changes for the punchline: the wee
Rabbi, still panting, like a startled boxer,

Looks at the dead one, then up at all those watching,
A kind of Mel Brooks gesture: "Hoo boy!" he says,
"Now that's what I call *really dead.*" O mortal

Powers and princes of earth, and you immortal
Lords of the underground and afterlife,
Jehovah, Raa, Bol-Morah, Hecate, Pluto,

What has a brilliant, living soul to do with
Your harps and fires and boats, your bric-a-brac
And troughs of smoking blood? Provincial stinkers,

Our languages don't touch you, you're like that mother
Whose small child entertained her to beg her life.
Possibly he grew up to be the tall rabbi,

The one who washed his hands of all those capers
Right at the outset. Or maybe he became
The author of these lines, a one-man *renga*

The one for whom it seems to be impossible
To tell a story straight. It was a routine
Procedure. When it was finished the physicians

Told Sandra and the kids it had succeeded.
But Elliot wouldn't wake up for maybe an hour.
They should go eat. The two of them loved to bicker

In a way that on his side went back to Yiddish,
On Sandra's to some Sicilian dialect.
He used to scold her endlessly for smoking.

When she got back from dinner with their children
The doctors had to tell them about the mistake.
Oh swirling petals, falling leaves! The movement

Of linking *renga* coursing from moment to moment
Is meaning, Bob says in his Haiku book.
Oh swirling petals, all living things are contingent,

Falling leaves, and transient, and they suffer.
But the Universal is the goal of jokes,
Especially certain ethnic jokes, which taper

Down through the swirling funnel of tongues and gestures
Toward their preposterous Ithaca. There's one
A journalist told me. He heard it while a hero

Of the South African freedom movement was speaking
To elderly Jews. The speaker's own right arm
Had been blown off by right-wing letter-bombers.

He told his listeners they had to cast their ballots
For the ANC—a group the old Jews feared
As "in with the Arabs." But they started weeping

As the old one-armed fighter told them their country
Needed them to vote for what was right, their vote
Could make a country their children could return to

From London and Chicago. The moved old people
Applauded wildly, and the speaker's friend
Whispered to the journalist, "It's the Belgian Army

Joke come to life." I wish that I could tell it
To Elliot. In the Belgian Army, the feud
Between the Flemings and Walloons grew vicious,

So out of hand the army could barely function.
Finally one commander assembled his men
In one great room, to deal with things directly.

They stood before him at attention. "All Flemings,"
He ordered, "to the left wall." Half the men
Clustered to the left. "Now all Walloons," he ordered,

"Move to the right." An equal number crowded
Against the right wall. Only one man remained
At attention in the middle: "What are you, soldier?"

Saluting, the man said, "Sir, I am a Belgian."
"Why, that's astonishing, Corporal—what's your name?"
Saluting again, "Rabinowitz," he answered:

A joke that seems at first to be a story
About the Jews. But as the *renga* describes
Religious meaning by moving in drifting petals

And brittle leaves that touch and die and suffer
The changing winds that riffle the gutter swirl,
So in the joke, just under the raucous music

Of Fleming, Jew, Walloon, a courtly allegiance
Moves to the dulcimer, gavotte and bow,
Over the banana tree the moon in autumn—

Allegiance to a state impossible to tell.

HEATHER McHUGH

Or Else

In memoriam: Mitchell Toney

What could we say to you
while you died? Could we
say "we"? Could we say "stay"?
(Who, after all, was moving?) My life was always

dealing in words, but now I'd better
listen, shut up and listen,
by the ditch of silver,
by the uninvested moon—all night among

the wealth of speechless
elements (where unlit earth
is dumbest): listen

for the shiver of a sign. Or else you die as surely
to, as from, us.

6.

"The Stained Stones":

Elegizing Those Dead by Violence

Wars and lynchings, genocides, assassinations, revolutions, and murders: violence begets countless bitter deaths and thus a host of embittered elegies. And though traditionally the war dead were honored, even envied, for their courageous demise, many nineteenth- and (especially) twentieth-century poets have deplored the brutal annihilation of soldiers on the battlefield as fiercely as they have lamented the extermination of hapless civilians on the home front or in concentration camps. "How sleep the brave who sink to rest / By all their country's wishes blest!" exclaimed the British poet William Collins in 1746, but by the time Elizabeth Barrett Browning was writing about the Italian *Risorgimento* in 1861, she assumed the persona of an Italian poet, Laura Savio, whose two sons were killed in the struggle, to declare roundly that if you "want a great song for your Italy free, / Let none look at *me!*"

Twentieth-century elegies for soldiers dead in the First and Second World Wars, along with laments for victims of lynching, of firebombing, of murder, of the Holocaust, of the conflict in Vietnam, and of the uprising in China's Tiananmen Square are even more scathing. "Red lips are not so red, / As the stained stones kissed by the English dead," insisted Wilfred Owen bitingly in a poem ironically entitled "Greater Love." Destined himself to die at the front in 1918, shortly before the Armistice, Owen joined other World War I participants (for example, Siegfried Sassoon and Ivor Gurney) in pioneering a genre of war poetry that was signally marked by what Jonathan Swift called "savage indignation." And other recorders of suffering, from African-Americans inveighing against lynching to Holocaust witnesses to Vietnam era activists expanded and enriched the genre.

Raged Langston Hughes in "Song for a Dark Girl,"

> Way Down South in Dixie
> (Break the heart of me)
> Love is a naked shadow
> On a gnarled and naked tree.

And in a similar mode, Naomi Replanski laments in "The Six Million," that during the Holocaust of World War II "No gods were there, no demons" but rather, more horrifyingly, the six million who died in the ovens of Auschwitz and Dachau

> . . . died at the hands of men,
> The cold that came from men,
> The lions made like men,
> The furnace built by men.

On a slightly different note, but just as intensely, Robert Bly suddenly decides, in "Driving through Minnesota during the Hanoi Bombings," that

> We were the ones we intended to bomb!
> Therefore we will have
> To go far away
> To atone. . . .

Yet to paraphrase a profound question about guilt and expiation once asked by T. S. Eliot—"After such knowledge, what forgiveness?"—most of the poems included in this section ask, implicitly or explicitly, "After such violence what atonement?"

WILLIAM COLLINS

Ode Written in the Beginning of the Year 1746

How sleep the brave who sink to rest
By all their country's wishes blest!
When Spring, with dewy fingers cold,
Returns to deck their hallowed mold,
She there shall dress a sweeter sod
Than Fancy's feet have ever trod.

By fairy hands their knell is rung,
By forms unseen their dirge is sung;
There Honor comes, a pilgrim gray,
To bless the turf that wraps their clay,
And Freedom shall awhile repair,
To dwell a weeping hermit there!

ELIZABETH BARRETT BROWNING

Mother and Poet

(Turin, After News from Gaeta, 1861)

1

Dead! One of them shot by the sea in the east,
    And one of them shot in the west by the sea.
Dead! both my boys! When you sit at the feast
    And are wanting a great song for Italy free,
Let none look at *me!*

2

Yet I was a poetess only last year,
    And good at my art, for a woman, men said;
But *this* woman, *this,* who is agonised here,
    —The east sea and west sea rhyme on in her head
      For ever instead.

3

What art can a woman be good at? Oh, vain!
    What art *is* she good at, but hurting her breast
With the milk-teeth of babes, and a smile at the pain?
    Ah boys, how you hurt! you were strong as you pressed,
      And I proud, by that test.

4

What art's for a woman? To hold on her knees
    Both darlings! to feel all their arms round her throat,
Cling, strangle a little! to sew by degrees
    And 'broider the long-clothes and neat little coat;
      To dream and to doat.

5

To teach them . . . It stings there! *I* made them indeed
   Speak plain the word *country*. I taught them, no doubt,
That a country's a thing men should die for at need.
   I prated of liberty, rights, and about
       The tyrant cast out.

6

And when their eyes flashed . . . O my beautiful eyes! . . .
   I exulted: nay, let them go forth at the wheels
Of the guns, and denied not. But then the surprise
   When one sits quite alone! Then one weeps, then one kneels!
       God, how the house feels!

7

At first, happy news came, in gay letters moiled
   With my kisses—of camp-life and glory, and how
They both loved me; and, soon coming home to be spoiled
   In return would fan off every fly from my brow
       With their green laurel-bough.

8

Then was triumph at Turin: "Ancona was free!"
   And some one came out of the cheers in the street,
With a face pale as stone, to say something to me.
   My Guido was dead! I fell down at his feet,
       While they cheered in the street.

9

I bore it; friends soothed me; my grief looked sublime
   As the ransom of Italy. One boy remained
To be leant on and walked with, recalling the time
   When the first grew immortal, while both of us strained
       To the height he had gained.

10

And letters still came, shorter, sadder, more strong,
  Writ now but in one hand. "I was not to faint,—
One loved me for two—would be with me ere long:
  And *Viva l'Italia!*—*he* died for, our saint,
    Who forbids our complaint."

11

My Nanni would add, "he was safe, and aware
  Of a presence that turned off the balls,—was imprest
It was Guido himself, who knew what I could bear,
  And how 'twas impossible, quite dispossessed
    To live on for the rest."

12

On which, without pause, up the telegraph line
  Swept smoothly the next news from Gaeta:—*Shot.*
Tell his mother. Ah, ah, "his," "their" mother,—not "mine,"
  No voice says "*My* mother" again to me. What!
    You think Guido forgot?

13

Are souls straight so happy that, dizzy with Heaven,
  They drop earth's affections, conceive not of woe?
I think not. Themselves were too lately forgiven
  Through THAT Love and Sorrow which reconciled so
    The Above and Below.

14

O Christ of the five wounds, who look'dst through the dark
  To the face of thy mother! consider, I pray,

How we common mothers stand desolate, mark,
  Whose sons, not being Christs, die with eyes turned away
    And no last word to say!

15

Both boys dead? but that's out of nature. We all
  Have been patriots, yet each house must always keep one.
'Twere imbecile, hewing out roads to a wall;
  And, when Italy's made, for what end is it done
    If we have not a son?

16

Ah, ah, ah! when Gaeta's taken, what then?
  When the fair wicked queen sits no more at her sport
Of the fire-balls of death crashing souls out of men?
  When the guns of Cavalli with final retort
    Have cut the game short?

17

When Venice and Rome keep their new jubilee,
  When your flag takes all heaven for its white, green, and red,
When you have your country from mountain to sea,
  When King Victor has Italy's crown on his head,
    (And *I* have my Dead)—

18

What then? Do not mock me. Ah, ring your bells low,
  And burn your lights faintly! *My* country is *there*,
Above the star pricked by the last peak of snow:
  My Italy's THERE, with my brave civic Pair,
    To disfranchise despair!

19

Forgive me. Some women bear children in strength,
  And bite back the cry of their pain in self-scorn;
But the birth-pangs of nations will wring us at length
  Into wail such as this—and we sit on forlorn
    When the man-child is born.

20

Dead! One of them shot by the sea in the east,
  And one of them shot in the west by the sea.
Both! both my boys! If in keeping the feast
  You want a great song for your Italy free,
    Let none look at *me!*

HERMAN MELVILLE

The Portent

(1859)

Hanging from the beam,
   Slowly swaying (such the law),

Gaunt the shadow on your green,
   Shenandoah!
The cut is on the crown
   (Lo, John Brown),
And the stabs shall heal no more.

Hidden in the cap
   Is the anguish none can draw;
So your future veils its face,
   Shenandoah!
But the streaming beard is shown
(Weird John Brown),
The meteor of the war.

ALICE MEYNELL

Parentage

"When Augustus Caesar legislated against the unmarried citizens of Rome, he declared them to be, in some sort, slayers of the people."

     Ah no! not these!
These, who were childless, are not they who gave
So many dead unto the journeying wave,
The helpless nurslings of the cradling seas;
Not they who doomed by infallible decrees
Unnumbered man to the innumerable grave.

     But those who slay
Are fathers. Theirs are armies. Death is theirs—
The death of innocences and despairs;
The dying of the golden and the gray.
The sentence, when these speak it, has no Nay.
And she who slays is she who bears, who bears.

RUDYARD KIPLING

from Epitaphs of the War

THE COWARD

I could not look on Death, which being known,
Men led me to him, blindfold and alone.

SHOCK

My name, my speech, my self I had forgot.
My wife and children came—I knew them not.
I died. My Mother followed. At her call
And on her bosom I remembered all.

BOMBED IN LONDON

On land and sea I strove with anxious care
To escape conscription. It was in the air!

BATTERIES OUT OF AMMUNITION

If any mourn us in the workshop, say
We died because the shift kept holiday.

COMMON FORM

If any question why we died,
Tell them, because our fathers lied.

DESTROYERS IN COLLISION

For Fog and Fate no charm is found
   To lighten or amend.
I, hurrying to my bride, was drowned—
   Cut down by my best friend.

EDGAR LEE MASTERS

Unknown Soldiers

Stranger! Tell the people of Spoon River two things:
First that we lie here, obeying their words;
And next that had we known what was back of their words
We should not be lying here!

EZRA POUND

from **Hugh Selwyn Mauberley**

<small>LIFE AND CONTACTS</small>
"Vocat æstus in umbram"[1]
—Nemesianus Ec. IV.

IV

These fought in any case,
and some believing,
           pro domo, in any case . . .

Some quick to arm,
some for adventure,
some from fear of weakness,
some from fear of censure,
some for love of slaughter, in imagination,
learning later . . .
some in fear, learning love of slaughter:

Died some, pro patria,
           non "dulce" non "et decor" . . .
walked eye-deep in hell
believing in old men's lies, then unbelieving
came home, home to a lie,
home to many deceits,
home to old lies and new infamy;
usury age-old and age-thick
and liars in public places.

Daring as never before, wastage as never before.
Young blood and high blood,

[1] "Summer heat calls us into the shade."

fair cheeks, and fine bodies;

fortitude as never before

frankness as never before,
disillusions as never told in the old days,
hysterias, trench confessions,
laughter out of dead bellies.

V

There died a myriad,
And of the best, among them,

For an old bitch gone in the teeth,
For a botched civilization,

Charm, smiling at the good mouth,
Quick eyes gone under earth's lid,

For two gross of broken statues,
For a few thousand battered books.

SIEGFRIED SASSOON

The General

"Good-morning; good-morning!" the General said
When we met him last week on our way to the line.
Now the soldiers he smiled at are most of 'em dead,
And we're cursing his staff for incompetent swine.
"He's a cheery old card," grunted Harry to Jack
As they slogged up to Arras with rifle and pack.

         .   .   .

But he did for them both by his plan of attack.

IVOR GURNEY

To His Love

He's gone, and all our plans
   Are useless indeed.
We'll walk no more on Cotswold
   Where the sheep feed
   Quietly and take no heed.

His body that was so quick
   Is not as you
Knew it, on Severn river
   Under the blue
   Driving our small boat through.

You would not know him now . . .
   But still he died
Nobly, so cover him over
   With violets of pride
   Purple from Severn side.

Cover him, cover him soon!
   And with thick-set
Masses of memoried flowers—
   Hide that red wet
   Thing I must somehow forget.

CLAUDE McKAY

The Lynching

His Spirit in smoke ascended to high heaven.
His father, by the cruelest way of pain,
Had bidden him to his bosom once again;
The awful sin remained still unforgiven.
All night a bright and solitary star
(Perchance the one that ever guided him,
Yet gave him up at last to Fate's wild whim)
Hung pitifully o'er the swinging char.
Day dawned, and soon the mixed crowds came to view
The ghastly body swaying in the sun.
The women thronged to look, but never a one
Showed sorrow in her eyes of steely blue.

And little lads, lynchers that were to be,
Danced round the dreadful thing in fiendish glee.

WILFRED OWEN

Anthem for Doomed Youth

What passing-bells for these who die as cattle?
   —Only the monstrous anger of the guns.
   Only the stuttering rifles' rapid rattle
Can patter out their hasty orisons.
No mockeries now for them; no prayers nor bells;
   Nor any voice of mourning save the choirs,—
The shrill, demented choirs of wailing shells;
   And bugles calling for them from sad shires.

What candles may be held to speed them all?
   Not in the hands of boys but in their eyes
Shall shine the holy glimmers of goodbyes.
   The pallor of girls' brows shall be their pall;
Their flowers the tenderness of patient minds,
And each slow dusk a drawing-down of blinds.

LANGSTON HUGHES

Song for a Dark Girl

Way Down South in Dixie
   (Break the heart of me)
They hung my black young lover
   To a cross roads tree.

Way Down South in Dixie
   (Bruised body high in air)
I asked the white Lord Jesus
   What was the use of prayer.

Way Down South in Dixie
   (Break the heart of me)
Love is a naked shadow
   On a gnarled and naked tree.

RICHARD EBERHART

The Fury of Aerial Bombardment

You would think the fury of aerial bombardment
Would rouse God to relent; the infinite spaces
Are still silent. He looks on shock-pried faces.
History, even, does not know what is meant.

You would feel that after so many centuries
God would give man to repent; yet he can kill
As Cain could, but with multitudinous will,
No farther advanced than in his ancient furies.

Was man made stupid to see his own stupidity?
Is God by definition indifferent, beyond us all?
Is the eternal truth man's fighting soul
Wherein the Beast ravens in its own avidity?

Of Van Wettering I speak, and Averill,
Names on a list, whose faces I do not recall
But they are gone to early death, who late in school
Distinguished the belt feed lever from the belt holding pawl.

ROBERT HAYDEN

Mourning Poem for the Queen of Sunday

Lord's lost Him His mockingbird,
His fancy warbler;
Satan sweet-talked her,
four bullets hushed her.
Who would have thought
she'd end that way?

Four bullets hushed her. And the world a-clang with evil.
Who's going to make old hardened sinner men tremble now
and the righteous rock?
Oh who and oh who will sing Jesus down
to help with struggling and doing without and being colored
all through blue Monday?
Till way next Sunday?

All those angels
in their cretonne clouds and finery
the true believer saw
when she rared back her head and sang,
all those angels are surely weeping.
Who would have thought
she'd end that way?

Four holes in her heart. The gold works wrecked.
But she looks so natural in her big bronze coffin
among the Broken Hearts and Gates-Ajar,
it's as if any moment she'd lift her head
from its pillow of chill gardenias
and turn this quiet into shouting Sunday
and make folks forget what she did on Monday.

Oh, Satan sweet-talked her,
and four bullets hushed her.
Lord's lost Him His diva,
His fancy warbler's gone.
Who would have thought,
who would have thought she'd end that way?

RANDALL JARRELL

The Death of the Ball Turret Gunner

From my mother's sleep I fell into the State,
And I hunched in its belly till my wet fur froze.
Six miles from earth, loosed from its dream of life,
I woke to black flak and the nightmare fighters.
When I died they washed me out of the turret with a hose.

The Six Million

They entered the fiery furnace
And never one came forth.
> How can that be, my brothers?
> No miracle, my sisters?
> They entered the fiery furnace
> And never one came forth.

They fell in the den of lions
Of lions made like men.
> No beast that wept, my brothers,
> Nor turned to lamb, my sisters.
> They fell in the den of lions
> Of lions made like men.

The block of ice closed round them
And nothing kept them warm.
> No gods came down, my brothers,
> To breathe on them, my sisters.
> The block of ice closed round them
> And nothing kept them warm.

No gods were there, no demons.
They died at the hands of men,
The cold that came from men,
The lions made like men,
The furnace built by men.
> How can that be, my brothers?
> But it is true, my sisters.
> No miracle to spare them,

No angel leaned upon them,
Their bodies made a mountain
That never touched the heavens.
Whose lightning struck the killers?
Whose rain drowned out the fires?

SHIRLEY KAUFMAN

After

We had been looking at an idol in a glass case,
size of a hand, admiring her tough little knobs
and the ball of her belly some barren woman
prayed to and rubbed. He said
she had been holding up her breasts
for eight thousand years.

Sun flickers through the pine trees,
my daughter beside me, we are crying
and holding each other, putting stones
on your daughter's grave.

After the flaming rib cage of the bus,
after each string of flesh has been found
and collected according to the Law,
after they show it and show it and show it
until we can smell the muck in our room
and the roasted skin, after the street
is washed clean with a blast of water,
and after the reading of the names,

there is absence, unreadable.

ROBERT BLY

Driving through Minnesota during the Hanoi Bombings

We drive between lakes just turning green;
Late June. The white turkeys have been moved
To new grass.
How long the seconds are in great pain!
Terror just before death,
Shoulders torn, shot
From helicopters, the boy
Tortured with the telephone generator,
"I felt sorry for him,
And blew his head off with a shotgun."
These instants become crystals,
Particles
The grass cannot dissolve. Our own gaiety
Will end up
In Asia, and in your cup you will look down
And see
Black Starfighters.
We were the ones we intended to bomb!
Therefore we will have
To go far away
To atone
For the sufferings of the stringy-chested
And the small rice-fed ones, quivering
In the helicopter like wild animals,
Shot in the chest, taken back to be questioned.

AUDRE LORDE

For the Record

in memory of Eleanor Bumpers

Call out the colored girls
and the ones who call themselves Black
and the ones who hate the word nigger
and the ones who are very pale

Who will count the big fleshy women
the grandmother weighing 22 stone
with the rusty braids
and a gap-toothed scowl
who wasn't afraid of Armageddon
the first shotgun blast tore her right arm off
the one with the butcher knife
the second blew out her heart
through the back of her chest
and I am going to keep writing it down
how they carried her body out of the house
dress torn   up around her waist
uncovered
past tenants and the neighborhood children
a mountain of Black Woman
and I am going to keep telling this
if it kills me
and it might in ways I am
learning

The next day Indira Gandhi
was shot down in her garden
and I wonder what these two 67-year-old
colored girls

are saying to each other now
planning their return
and they weren't even
sisters.

WILLIAM HEYEN

Blue

They were burning something. A lorry drew up at the pit and delivered its load—
little children. Babies! Yes, I saw it—saw it with my own eyes . . . those children
in the flames. . . . I pinched my face. Was I still alive? Was I awake? I could not
believe it. . . . Never shall I forget the little faces of the children, whose bodies I
saw turned into wreaths of smoke, beneath a silent blue sky.
—Elie Wiesel

To witness, to
enter this
essence, this
silence, this
blue, color
of sky, wreaths
of smoke, bodies
of children blue
in their nets
of veins: a lorry
draws up at the pit
under the blue sky where
wreaths rise. These
are the children's bodies, this
our earth. Blue. A lorry
draws up at the pit
where children smolder. The sky
deepens into blue, its
meditation, a blue
flame, the children
smolder. Lord of blue,
blue chest and blue brain,
a lorry of murdered children
draws up at the pit. This
happened, this
happens, Your
sign, children
flaming in their rags, children
of bone-smolder, scroll
of wreaths on Your blue
bottomless sky, children
rising wreathed
to Your blue lips

YUSEF KOMUNYAKAA

Facing It

My black face fades,
hiding inside the black granite.
I said I wouldn't,
dammit: No tears.
I'm stone. I'm flesh.
My clouded reflection eyes me
like a bird of prey, the profile of night
slanted against morning. I turn
this way—the stone lets me go.
I turn that way—I'm inside
the Vietnam Veterans Memorial
again, depending on the light
to make a difference.
I go down the 58,022 names,
half-expecting to find
my own in letters like smoke.
I touch the name Andrew Johnson;
I see the booby trap's white flash.
Names shimmer on a woman's blouse
but when she walks away
the names stay on the wall.
Brushstrokes flash, a red bird's
wings cutting across my stare.
The sky. A plane in the sky.
A white vet's image floats
closer to me, then his pale eyes
look through mine. I'm a window.
He's lost his right arm
inside the stone. In the black mirror
a woman's trying to erase names:
No, she's brushing a boy's hair.

JAMES FENTON

Tiananmen

Tiananmen
Is broad and clean
And you can't tell
Where the dead have been
And you can't tell
What happened then
And you can't speak
Of Tiananmen.

You must not speak.
You must not think.
You must not dip
Your brush in ink.
You must not say
What happened then,
What happened there
In Tiananmen.

The cruel men
Are old and deaf
Ready to kill
But short of breath
And they will die
Like other men
And they'll lie in state
In Tiananmen.

They lie in state.
They lie in style.
Another lie's
Thrown on the pile,

Thrown on the pile
By the cruel men
To cleanse the blood
From Tiananmen.

Truth is a secret.
Keep it dark.
Keep it dark
In your heart of hearts.
Keep it dark
Till you know when
Truth may return
To Tiananmen.

Tiananmen
Is broad and clean
And you can't tell
Where the dead have been
And you can't tell
When they'll come again.
They'll come again
To Tiananmen.

7.

"Brightness Falls from the Air":

Grieving for the Great and Beautiful

There is a special quality of incredulity that we bring to our grief for the great and beautiful, the famous, wise, and powerful, for many of us regard strong statesmen, splendid athletes, brilliant thinkers, and glamorous actresses—along with other celebrities—not just as heroes and heroines, but as virtually gods and goddesses. How, then, can such figures be so frail as to die? And if they, with their strength or beauty, fame or wisdom, can die, how much more vulnerable are we ourselves! "Brightness falls from the air, / Queens have died young and fair. . . . Strength stoops unto the grave, / Worms feed on Hector brave": so wrote Thomas Nashe in the Elizabethan "Litany in Time of Plague," a meditation on mortality included in Section 10 of this book. But note how surprising it seems, even to this bitterly philosophical poet, that strength and beauty, traits often imputed to the divine, are in fact inexorably mortal.

Some elegies for great or celebrated people are as generalized as Nashe's comments on "Queens" or on the mythical "Hector brave." A. E. Housman's "To an Athlete Dying Young" and Edwin Arlington Robinson's "For a Dead Lady" name no names; rather, they merely mourn the doom of the qualities that distinguished their subjects. But often the most effective elegies speak to and of specific people, even while they also grieve the fate that must overtake all persons. Thus, in "When Lilacs Last in the Dooryard Bloom'd"—one of the most beautiful and resonant elegies ever written—Walt Whitman laments the particular death of Abraham Lincoln, whom he considered "the sweetest, wisest soul of all my days and lands," but also confesses that in mourning the assassinated president he is addressing "the coffins all of you O death."

WALT WHITMAN

When Lilacs Last in the Dooryard Bloom'd

1

When lilacs last in the dooryard bloom'd,
And the great star early droop'd in the western sky in the night,
I mourn'd, and yet shall mourn with ever-returning spring.

Ever-returning spring, trinity sure to me you bring,
Lilac blooming perennial and drooping star in the west,
And thought of him I love.

2

O powerful western fallen star!
O shades of night—O moody, tearful night!
O great star disappear'd—O the black murk that hides the star!
O cruel hands that hold me powerless—O helpless soul of me!
O harsh surrounding cloud that will not free my soul.

3

In the dooryard fronting an old farm-house near the white-wash'd palings,
Stands the lilac-bush tall-growing with heart-shaped leaves of rich green,
With many a pointed blossom rising delicate, with the perfume strong
    I love,
With every leaf a miracle—and from this bush in the dooryard,
With delicate-color'd blossoms and heart-shaped leaves of rich green,
A sprig with its flower I break.

4

In the swamp in secluded recesses,
A shy and hidden bird is warbling a song.

Solitary the thrush,
The hermit withdrawn to himself, avoiding the settlements,
Sings by himself a song.

Song of the bleeding throat,
Death's outlet song of life, (for well dear brother I know,
If thou wast not granted to sing thou would'st surely die.)

5

Over the breast of the spring, the land, amid cities,
Amid lanes and through old woods, where lately the violets peep'd
    from the ground, spotting the gray debris,
Amid the grass in the fields each side of the lanes, passing the endless
    grass,
Passing the yellow-spear'd wheat, every grain from its shroud in the
    dark-brown fields uprisen,
Passing the apple-tree blows of white and pink in the orchards,
Carrying a corpse to where it shall rest in the grave,
Night and day journeys a coffin.

6

Coffin that passes through lanes and streets,
Through day and night with the great cloud darkening the land,
With the pomp of the inloop'd flags with the cities draped in black,
With the show of the States themselves as of crape-veil'd women
    standing,
With processions long and winding and the flambeaus of the night,
With the countless torches lit, with the silent sea of faces and the un-
    bared heads,
With the waiting depot, the arriving coffin, and the sombre faces,
With dirges through the night, with the thousand voices rising strong
    and solemn,
With all the mournful voices of the dirges pour'd around the coffin,
The dim-lit churches and the shuddering organs—where amid these
    you journey,

With the tolling tolling bells' perpetual clang,
Here, coffin that slowly passes,
I give you my sprig of lilac.

7

(Nor for you, for one alone,
Blossoms and branches green to coffins all I bring,
For fresh as the morning, thus would I chant a song for you O sane and
    sacred death.

All over bouquets of roses,
O death, I cover you over with roses and early lilies,
But mostly and now the lilac that blooms the first,
Copious I break, I break the sprigs from the bushes,
With loaded arms I come, pouring for you,
For you and the coffins all of you O death.)

8

O western orb sailing the heaven,
Now I know what you must have meant as a month since I walk'd,
As I walk'd in silence the transparent shadowy night,
As I saw you had something to tell as you bent to me night after night,
As you droop'd from the sky low down as if to my side, (while the other
    stars all look'd on,)
As we wander'd together the solemn night, (for something I know not
    what kept me from sleep,)
As the night advanced, and I saw on the rim of the west how full you
    were of woe,
As I stood on the rising ground in the breeze in the cool transparent
    night,
As I watch'd where you pass'd and was lost in the netherward black of
    the night,
As my soul in its trouble dissatisfied sank, as where you sad orb,
Concluded, dropt in the night, and was gone.

9

Sing on there in the swamp,
O singer bashful and tender, I hear your notes, I hear your call,
I hear, I come presently, I understand you,
But a moment I linger, for the lustrous star has detain'd me,
The star my departing comrade holds and detains me.

10

O how shall I warble myself for the dead one there I loved?
And how shall I deck my song for the large sweet soul that has gone?
And what shall my perfume be for the grave of him I love?

Sea-winds blown from east and west,
Blown from the Eastern sea and blown from the Western sea, till there
    on the prairies meeting,
These and with these and the breath of my chant,
I'll perfume the grave of him I love.

11

O what shall I hang on the chamber walls?
And what shall the pictures be that I hang on the walls,
To adorn the burial-house of him I love?

Pictures of growing spring and farms and homes,
With the Fourth-month eve at sundown, and the gray smoke lucid and
    bright,
With floods of the yellow gold of the gorgeous, indolent, sinking sun,
    burning, expanding the air,
With the fresh sweet herbage under foot, and the pale green leaves of
    the trees prolific,
In the distance the flowing glaze, the broast of the river, with a wind-
    dapple here and there,

With ranging hills on the banks, with many a line against the sky, and
    shadows,
And the city at hand with dwellings so dense, and stacks of chimneys,
And all the scenes of life and the workshops, and the workmen home-
    ward returning.

12

Lo, body and soul—this land,
My own Manhattan with spires, and the sparkling and hurrying tides,
    and the ships,
The varied and ample land, the South and the North in the light,
    Ohio's shores and flashing Missouri,
And ever the far-spreading prairies cover'd with grass and corn.

Lo, the most excellent sun so calm and haughty,
The violet and purple morn with just-felt breezes,
The gentle soft-born measureless light,
The miracle spreading bathing all, the fulfill'd noon,
The coming eve delicious, the welcome night and the stars,
Over my cities shining all, enveloping man and land.

13

Sing on, sing on you gray-brown bird,
Sing from the swamps, the recesses, pour your chant from the bushes,
Limitless out of the dusk, out of the cedars and pines.

Sing on dearest brother, warble your reedy song,
Loud human song, with voice of uttermost woe.

O liquid and free and tender!
O wild and loose to my soul!—O wondrous singer!
You only I hear—yet the star holds me, (but will soon depart,)
Yet the lilac with mastering odor holds me.

Now while I sat in the day and look'd forth,
In the close of the day with its light and the fields of spring, and the
    farmers preparing their crops,
In the large unconscious scenery of my land with its lakes and forests,
In the heavenly aerial beauty, (after the perturb'd winds and the storms,)
Under the arching heavens of the afternoon swift passing, and the
    voices of children and women,
The many-moving sea-tides, and I saw the ships how they sail'd,
And the summer approaching with richness, and the fields all busy
    with labor,
And the infinite separate houses, how they all went on, each with its
    meals and minutia of daily usages,
And the streets how their throbbings throbb'd, and the cities pent—lo,
    then and there,
Falling upon them all and among them all, enveloping me with the rest,
Appear'd the cloud, appear'd the long black trail,
And I knew death, its thought, and the sacred knowledge of death.

Then with the knowledge of death as walking one side of me,
And the thought of death close-walking the other side of me,
And I in the middle as with companions, and as holding the hands of
    companions,
I fled forth to the hiding receiving night that talks not,
Down to the shores of the water, the path by the swamp in the dimness,
To the solemn shadowy cedars and ghostly pines so still.

And the singer so shy to the rest receiv'd me,
The gray-brown bird I know receiv'd us comrades three,
And he sang the carol of death, and a verse for him I love.

From deep secluded recesses,
From the fragrant cedars and the ghostly pines so still,
Came the carol of the bird.

And the charm of the carol rapt me,
As I held as if by their hands my comrades in the night,
And the voice of my spirit tallied the song of the bird.

Come lovely and soothing death,
Undulate round the world, serenely arriving, arriving,
In the day, in the night, to all, to each,
Sooner or later delicate death.

Prais'd be the fathomless universe,
For life and joy, and for objects and knowledge curious,
And for love, sweet love—but praise! praise! praise!
For the sure-enwinding arms of cool-enfolding death.

Dark mother always gliding near with soft feet,
Have none chanted for thee a chant of fullest welcome?
Then I chant it for thee, I glorify thee above all,
I bring thee a song that when thou must indeed come, come unfalteringly.

Approach strong deliveress,
When it is so, when thou hast taken them I joyously sing the dead,
Lost in the loving floating ocean of thee,
Laved in the flood of thy bliss O death.

From me to thee glad serenades,
Dances for thee I propose saluting thee, adornments and feastings for thee,
And the sights of the open landscape and the high-spread sky are fitting,
And life and the fields, and the huge and thoughtful night.

The night in silence under many a star,
The ocean shore and the husky whispering wave whose voice I know,
And the soul turning to thee O vast and well-veil'd death,
And the body gratefully nestling close to thee.

Over the tree-tops I float thee a song,
Over the rising and sinking waves, over the myriad fields and the prairies
    wide,
Over the dense-pack'd cities all and the teeming wharves and ways,
I float this carol with joy, with joy to thee O death.

15

To the tally of my soul,
Loud and strong kept up the gray-brown bird,
With pure deliberate notes spreading filling the night.

Loud in the pines and cedars dim,
Clear in the freshness moist and the swamp-perfume,
And I with my comrades there in the night.

While my sight that was bound in my eyes unclosed,
As to long panoramas of visions.

And I saw askant the armies,
I saw as in noiseless dreams hundreds of battle-flags,
Borne through the smoke of the battles and pierc'd with missiles I saw
    them,
And carried hither and yon through the smoke, and torn and bloody,
And at last but a few shreds left on the staffs, (and all in silence,)
And the staffs all splinter'd and broken.

I saw battle-corpses, myriads of them,
And the white skeletons of young men, I saw them,
I saw the debris and debris of all the slain soldiers of the war,
But I saw they were not as was thought,
They themselves were fully at rest, they suffer'd not,
The living remain'd and suffer'd, the mother suffer'd,
And the wife and the child and the musing comrade suffer'd,
And the armies that remain'd suffer'd.

16

Passing the visions, passing the night,
Passing, unloosing the hold of my comrades' hands,
Passing the song of the hermit bird and the tallying song of my soul,
Victorious song, death's outlet song, yet varying ever-altering song,

As low and wailing, yet clear the notes, rising and falling, flooding the
   night,
Sadly sinking and fainting, as warning and warning, and yet again
   bursting with joy,
Covering the earth and filling the spread of the heaven,
As that powerful psalm in the night I heard from recesses,
Passing, I leave thee lilac with heart-shaped leaves,
I leave thee there in the door-yard, blooming, returning with spring.

I cease from my song for thee,
From my gaze on thee in the west, fronting the west, communing with
   thee,
O comrade lustrous with silver face in the night.

Yet each to keep and all, retrievements out of the night,
The song, the wondrous chant of the gray-brown bird,
And the tallying chant, the echo arous'd in my soul,
With the lustrous and drooping star with the countenance full of woe,
With the holders holding my hand nearing the call of the bird,
Comrades mine and I in the midst, and their memory ever to keep, for
   the dead I loved so well,
For the sweetest, wisest soul of all my days and lands—and this for his
   dear sake,
Lilac and star and bird twined with the chant of my soul,
There in the fragrant pines and the cedars dusk and dim.

A. E. HOUSMAN

To an Athlete Dying Young

The time you won your town the race
We chaired you through the market-place;
Man and boy stood cheering by,
And home we brought you shoulder-high.

To-day, the road all runners come,
Shoulder-high we bring you home,
And set you at your threshold down,
Townsman of a stiller town.

Smart lad, to slip betimes away
From fields where glory does not stay
And early though the laurel grows
It withers quicker than the rose.

Eyes the shady night has shut
Cannot see the record cut,
And silence sounds no worse than cheers
After earth has stopped the ears:

Now you will not swell the rout
Of lads that wore their honours out,
Runners whom renown outran
And the name died before the man.

So set, before its echoes fade,
The fleet foot on the sill of shade,
And hold to the low lintel up
The still-defended challenge-cup.

And round that early-laurelled head
Will flock to gaze the strengthless dead
And find unwithered on its curls
The garland briefer than a girl's.

EDWIN ARLINGTON ROBINSON

For a Dead Lady

No more with overflowing light
Shall fill the eyes that now are faded,
Nor shall another's fringe with night
Their woman-hidden world as they did.
No more shall quiver down the days
The flowing wonder of her ways,
Whereof no language may requite
The shifting and the many-shaded.

The grace, divine, definitive,
Clings only as a faint forestalling;
The laugh that love could not forgive
Is hushed, and answers to no calling;
The forehead and the little ears
Have gone where Saturn keeps the years;
The breast where roses could not live
Has done with rising and with falling.

The beauty, shattered by the laws
That have creation in their keeping,
No longer trembles at applause,
Or over children that are sleeping;
And we who delve in beauty's lore
Know all that we have known before
Of what inexorable cause
Makes Time so vicious in his reaping.

E. E. CUMMINGS

Buffalo Bill's Lament

from Portraits

VIII

Buffalo Bill's
defunct
            who used to
            ride a watersmooth-silver
                                    stallion
and break onetwothreefourfive pigeonsjustlikethat
                                                Jesus
he was a handsome man
                        and what i want to know is
how do you like your blueeyed boy
Mister Death

FRANK O'HARA

The Day Lady Died

It is 12:20 in New York a Friday
three days after Bastille day, yes
it is 1959 and I go get a shoeshine
because I will get off the 4:19 in Easthampton
at 7:15 and then go straight to dinner
and I don't know the people who will feed me

I walk up the muggy street beginning to sun
and have a hamburger and a malted and buy
an ugly NEW WORLD WRITING to see what the poets
in Ghana are doing these days
                    I go on to the bank
and Miss Stillwagon (first name Linda I once heard)
doesn't even look up my balance for once in her life
and in the GOLDEN GRIFFIN I get a little Verlaine
for Patsy with drawings by Bonnard although I do
think of Hesiod, trans. Richmond Lattimore or
Brendan Behan's new play or *Le Balcon* or *Les Nègres*
of Genet, but I don't, I stick with Verlaine
after practically going to sleep with quandariness

and for Mike I just stroll into the PARK LANE
Liquor Store and ask for a bottle of Strega and
then I go back where I came from to 6th Avenue
and the tobacconist in the Ziegfeld Theatre and
casually ask for a carton of Gauloises and a carton
of Picayunes, and a NEW YORK POST with her face on it

and I am sweating a lot by now and thinking of
leaning on the john door in the 5 SPOT
while she whispered a song along the keyboard
to Mal Waldron and everyone and I stopped breathing

LUCILLE CLIFTON

malcolm

nobody mentioned war
but doors were closed
black women shaved their heads
black men rustled in the alleys like leaves
prophets were ambushed as they spoke
and from their holes black eagles flew
screaming through the streets

BETTY ADCOCK

Poem for Dizzy

written after discovering that
no poem in The Anthology of Jazz
Poetry *is written to, for, or about*
Dizzy Gillespie, who was cocreator
(with Charlie Parker) of bebop,
the style that ushered in the modern
jazz era

Sweet and sly, you were all business when the old bent-
skyward horn went up. Sometimes it went up like a rocket,
sometimes like a gentle-turning lark
high on a summer day. It could blow an island wind
snapping a line of red and yellow clothes
hard against blue.
The breath pouring into that banged-up
brass inclination heavenward
gave us lesson number one: *Be.*
Lesson number two came naturally.

And you were serious as sunrise. Those who scoffed
or bristled at the little stageside dance,
the cutting-up, the jokes and jive, have all gone off
to other targets. And you, Dizzy,
you've gone off too, asleep in your chair,
leaving us bereft. There was nobody better.

But there were lives the poets would want more—
for tragedy or politics, harsher
experiments: Bird's drugged vortex into gone,
Coltrane's absolute, Monk's edgy monologues, the demon
Miles Davis posed as, then became.

But you played clown, put everybody on.
You played the house, but played a soul into the horn.
And you outlived them all. This too was real jazz.

Talking, you were evasive, slant as a riff
around a melody, more private maybe
than anybody knew. I remember your one week
in our town, 1970:
afternoons you'd wander with your camera.
Putting his flute back in its case, Moody told us:
He does that every place we go, walks around
for hours by himself, just taking pictures
of wherever it is he is. Lesson number one.

You looked like the face of South Wind
in my childhood picture book,
like the best cherub
Italy ever chiseled above a doge
or saint, rich man, or pope.
What were you storing in those blown-out cheeks
all the years? Your darkest jokes?
some brand-new pure invention, notes
outside our hearing? Or perhaps some simple tune
we'd never have made much sense of,
the one about hope. The one about oldest love.

RICHARD BLESSING

Elegy for Elvis

August, 1977

Elvis lay cool in his thick shadow
and saw it was an island no one
would come to ever again. It was Memphis
and summer. It was winter. Snow was falling
blue as Christmas. It was so still
he heard his heart fill like a lonesome hotel.

Listen, John Berryman used to like to say,
Whyncha ask me whattis like to be famous?
What did he know, King? What did he know?
He never sold a million. When he died
not many women looked at their lives
like closets of spikes and pointy toes
and asked, *What good is any of it now?*

Dr. Nichopoulous was saying, *Come on, Presley,*
breathe for me, but you were happy. You'd played
your last request. Snow settled around you
like a thousand paternity suits. Ice
filled the island trees. You had gone farther
than a gossip magazine. You planned to name
your shadow for the first American to say,
I never heard of him.

Presley, you always breathed for me,
rock-bellied, up from Tupelo, a place

pastoral enough for elegy. Now one of us
is dead. Tender as Whitman's lilac sprig,
I leave these plastic flowers in the snow.
What perishes is only really real.
I twist the dial and you are everywhere.

SHARON OLDS

The Death of Marilyn Monroe

The ambulance men touched her cold
body, lifted it, heavy as iron,
onto the stretcher, tried to close
the mouth, closed the eyes, tied the
arms to the side, moved a caught
strand of hair, as if it mattered,
saw the shape of her breasts, flattened by
gravity, under the sheet,
carried her, as if it were she,
down the steps.

These men were never the same. They went out
afterwards, as they always did,
for a drink or two, but they could not meet
each other's eyes.

          Their lives took
a turn—one had nightmares, strange
pains, impotence, depression. One did not
like his work, his wife looked
different, his kids. Even death
seemed different to him—a place where she
would be waiting,

and one found himself standing at night
in the doorway to a room of sleep, listening to a
woman breathing, just an ordinary
woman
breathing.

RITA DOVE

Sonnet in Primary Colors

This is for the woman with one black wing
perched over her eyes: lovely Frida, erect
among parrots, in the stern petticoats of the peasant,
who painted herself a present—
wildflowers entwining the plaster corset
her spine resides in, that flaming pillar—
this priestess in the romance of mirrors.

Each night she lay down in pain and rose
to the celluloid butterflies of her Beloved Dead,
Lenin and Marx and Stalin arrayed at the footstead.
And rose to her easel, the hundred dogs panting
like children along the graveled walks of the garden, Diego's
love a skull in the circular window
of the thumbprint searing her immutable brow.

8.

"Laments for the Makers":

Poets Mourning Other Poets

From the fifteenth-century Scottish poet William Dunbar to the contemporary American poet W. S. Merwin, "makers" of verse have lamented the loss of fellow makers, singling out specific highly respected artists as objects of special veneration—and special grief. Many of the most impassioned elegies in this mode are dedicated to poets who were intimate friends of the writer. Thus Ben Jonson memorializes Shakespeare, his comrade in the London theatre, while Maxine Kumin mourns her close friend and sister-poet Anne Sexton, and Sexton herself grieves for another companion-in-verse, Sylvia Plath. Even when there was no actual personal relationship between two poets, however, the one often mourns the other as a like member of that guild of aesthetic craftspersons to which all artists belong. Wordsworth, for instance, grieves for the absence of John Milton while invoking Milton's spirit, and similarly Emily Dickinson laments the death of Elizabeth Barrett Browning while celebrating Barrett Browning's final achievements.

Sometimes, to be sure, a note of awe-struck rivalry steals into these verses, as when John Berryman declares to the ghost of William Butler Yeats that "I have moved to Dublin to have it out with you, / majestic Shade." But more often the tone of such laments for the makers is one of respectful gratitude, as when Christopher Gilbert reverently describes the words of his onetime writing teacher, Robert Hayden, "breaking in flower," and notes that therefore "the breath on things" wears "bright new clothes."

WILLIAM DUNBAR

Lament for the Makaris[1]

I that in heill° was and gladness,   *health*
Am troublit now with great seikness,°   *sickness*
And feeblit with infirmity:
    Timor Mortis conturbat me.[2]

Our plesance here is all vain-glory
This false warld is bot transitory,
The flesh is brukill,° the Fiend is sle;°   *frail / sly*
    Timor Mortis conturbat me.

The state of man dois change and vary,
Now sound, now seik, now blyth,° now sary,°   *happy / sorry*
Now dansand merry, now like to die;[3]
    Timor Mortis conturbat me.

No state in erd° here standis siccar;°   *earth / securely*
As with the wind wavis° the wicker,°   *waves / willow*
Wavis this warldis vanitie;
    Timor Mortis conturbat me.

Unto the deid gois all Estatis,
Princes, Prelatis,° and Potestatis,°   *prelates / potentates*
Baith rich and puir° of all degree;   *poor*
    Timor Mortis conturbat me.

He takes the knichtis into the field,
Enarmit under helm and shield;

---

[1] poets

[2] "The fear of death dismays me" (Latin); a line from the Office of the Dead.

[3] i.e., now dance and be merry, now likely to die

Victor he is at all mêlée;°   *battles*
    Timor Mortis conturbat me.

That strang° unmerciful tyrand   *strong*
Takis on the moderis breist soukand°   *sucking*
The babe, full of benignite;°   *gentleness*
    Timor Mortis conturbat me.

He takis the champion in the stour,°   *battle*
The capitane closit in the tour,°   *tower*
The lady in bour° full of beautie;   *bedroom*
    Timor Mortis conturbat me.

He sparis no lord for his puissance,
Na clerk° for his intelligence;   *scholar*
His awful straik° may no man flee;   *stroke*
    Timor Mortis conturbat me.

Art magicianis,[4] and astrologis,°   *astrologers*
Rethoris,° logicianis, and theologis,   *rhetoricians*
Them helpis no conclusionis sle;°   *sly, clever*
    Timor Mortis conturbat me.

In medicine the most° practicianis,   *greatest*
Leechis,° surigianis, and phisicianis,   *doctors*
Them-self fra deid° may not supple;°   *death / help*
    Timor Mortis conturbat me.

I see that makaris amang the lave°   *remainder*
Playis here their pageant, syne° gois to grave;   *then*
Sparit° is nocht° their facultie;   *spared / not*
    Timor Mortis conturbat me.

[4] those practicing the art of magic

He has done piteously devour
The noble Chaucer, of makaris flour,°   *flower*
The Monk of Bery, and Gower, all three;
   Timor Mortis conturbat me.

The gude Sir Hew of Eglintoun,[5]
And eik° Heriot, and Wintoun,   *also*
He has ta'en out of this countrie;
   Timor Mortis conturbat me.

That scorpion fell has done infec'°   *infected*
Maister John Clerk and James Affleck,
Fra ballad-making and tragedie;
   Timor Mortis conturbat me.

Holland and Barbour he has bereavit;
Alas! that he nought with us leavit
Sir Mungo Lockhart of the Lea;
   Timor Mortis conturbat me.

Clerk of Tranent eke he has ta'en,
That made the Aunteris° of Gawain,   *adventures*
Sir Gilbert Hay endit has he;
   Timor Mortis conturbat me.

He has Blind Harry, and Sandy Traill
Slain with his shour° of mortal hail,   *shower*
Whilk° Patrick Johnstoun micht nocht flee;   *which*
   Timor Mortis conturbat me.

He has reft Merser endite,[6]
That did in luve so lively write,
So short, so quick, of sentence hie;°   *lively*
   Timor Mortis conturbat me.

[5] the first in a list of Scots poets, some well known, some obscure
[6] i.e., Death has taken the practice of poetry from Mercer.

He has ta'en Roull of Aberdeen,
And gentle Roull of Corstorphin;
Two better fellowis did no man see;
  Timor Mortis conturbat me.

In Dunfermline he has done roune°   *made a circuit*
With Maister Robert Henryson;
Sir John the Ross embraced has he;
  Timor Mortis conturbat me.

And he has now ta'en, last of a',
Gude gentle Stobo and Quintin Shaw,
Of wham all wichtis° has pitie: *creatures*
  Timor Mortis conturbat me.

Gude Maister Walter Kennedy
In point of deid lies verily,
Great ruth° it were that so suld be;   *pity*
  Timor Mortis conturbat me.

Sen he has all my brether° ta'en,   *brothers*
He will nocht lat me live alane,
On force I maun° his next prey be;   *must*
  Timor Mortis conturbat me.

Sen for the deid remead° is none,   *remedy*
Best is that we for deid dispone,°   *prepare*
Eftir our deid that live may we;
  Timor Mortis conturbat me.

BEN JONSON

To the Memory of My Beloved, The Author, Mr. William Shakespeare, and What He Hath Left Us

To draw no envy, Shakespeare, on thy name
  Am I thus ample to thy book and fame,
While I confess thy writings to be such
  As neither man nor Muse can praise too much.
'Tis true, and all men's suffrage. But these ways
  Were not the paths I meant unto thy praise;
For silliest ignorance on these may light,
  Which, when it sounds at best, but echoes right;
Or blind affection, which doth ne'er advance
  The truth, but gropes, and urgeth all by chance;
Or crafty malice might pretend this praise,
  And think to ruin where it seemed to raise.
These are as some infamous bawd or whore
  Should praise a matron. What could hurt her more?
But thou art proof against them, and, indeed,
  Above th' ill fortune of them, or the need.
I therefore will begin. Soul of the age!
  The applause! delight! the wonder of our stage!
My Shakespeare, rise; I will not lodge thee by
  Chaucer or Spenser, or bid Beaumont lie
A little further to make thee a room:
  Thou art a monument without a tomb,
And art alive still while thy book doth live,
  And we have wits to read and praise to give.
That I not mix thee so, my brain excuses,
  I mean with great, but disproportioned Muses;
For, if I thought my judgment were of years,
  I should commit thee surely with thy peers,
And tell how far thou didst our Lyly outshine,
  Or sporting Kyd, or Marlowe's mighty line.

And though thou hadst small Latin and less Greek,
    From thence to honor thee I would not seek
For names, but call forth thund'ring Aeschylus,
    Euripides, and Sophocles to us,
Pacuvius, Accius, him of Cordova dead,
    To life again, to hear thy buskin tread
And shake a stage; or, when thy socks were on,
    Leave thee alone for the comparison
Of all that insolent Greece or haughty Rome
    Sent forth, or since did from their ashes come.
Triumph, my Britain; thou hast one to show
    To whom all scenes of Europe homage owe.
He was not of an age, but for all time!
    And all the Muses still were in their prime
When like Apollo he came forth to warm
    Our ears, or like a Mercury to charm.
Nature herself was proud of his designs,
    And joyed to wear the dressing of his lines,
Which were so richly spun, and woven so fit,
    As, since, she will vouchsafe no other wit:
The merry Greek, tart Aristophanes,
    Neat Terence, witty Plautus now not please,
But antiquated and deserted lie,
    As they were not of Nature's family.
Yet must I not give Nature all; thy Art,
    My gentle Shakespeare, must enjoy a part.
For though the poet's matter Nature be,
    His Art doth give the fashion, and that he
Who casts to write a living line must sweat
    (Such as thine are) and strike the second heat
Upon the muses' anvil; turn the same,
    And himself with it, that he thinks to frame,
Or for the laurel he may gain a scorn;
    For a good poet's made as well as born
And such wert thou! Look how the father's face
    Lives in his issue; even so the race

Of Shakespeare's mind and manners brightly shines
    In his well-turned and true-filed lines,
In each of which he seems to shake a lance,
    As brandished at the eyes of ignorance.
Sweet swan of Avon, what a sight it were
    To see thee in our waters yet appear,
And make those flights upon the banks of Thames
    That so did take Eliza and our James!
But stay; I see thee in the hemisphere
    Advanced and made a constellation there!
Shine forth, thou star of poets, and with rage
    Or influence chide or cheer the drooping stage,
Which, since thy flight from hence, hath mourned like night,
    And despairs day, but for thy volume's light.

WILLIAM WORDSWORTH

London, 1802

Milton! thou should'st be living at this hour:
England hath need of thee: she is a fen
Of stagnant waters: altar, sword, and pen,
Fireside, the heroic wealth of hall and bower,
Have forfeited their ancient English dower
Of inward happiness. We are selfish men;
Oh! raise us up, return to us again;
And give us manners, virtue, freedom, power.
Thy soul was like a Star, and dwelt apart:
Thou hadst a voice whose sound was like the sea:
Pure as the naked heavens, majestic, free,
So didst thou travel on life's common way,
In cheerful godliness; and yet thy heart
The lowliest duties on herself did lay.

EMILY DICKINSON

Her — "last Poems" — (#600)

Her — "last Poems" —
Poets — ended —
Silver — perished — with her Tongue —
Not on Record — bubbled other,
Flute — or Woman —
So divine —
Not unto its Summer — Morning
Robin — uttered Half the Tune —
Gushed too free for the Adoring —
From the Anglo-Florentine —
Late — the Praise —
'Tis dull — conferring
On the Head too High to Crown —
Diadem — or Ducal Showing —
Be its Grave — sufficient sign —
Nought — that We — No Poet's Kinsman —
Suffocate — with easy woe —
What, and if, Ourself a Bridegroom —
Put Her down — in Italy?

HART CRANE

At Melville's Tomb

Often beneath the wave, wide from this ledge
The dice of drowned men's bones he saw bequeath
An embassy. Their numbers as he watched,
Beat on the dusty shore and were obscured.

And wrecks passed without sound of bells,
The calyx of death's bounty giving back
A scattered chapter, livid hieroglyph,
The portent wound in corridors of shells.

Then in the circuit calm of one vast coil,
Its lashings charmed and malice reconciled,
Frosted eyes there were that lifted altars,
And silent answers crept across the stars.

Compass, quadrant and sextant contrive
No farther tides . . . High in the azure steeps
Monody shall not wake the mariner.
This fabulous shadow only the sea keeps.

ELIZABETH BISHOP

North Haven

In memoriam: Robert Lowell

I can make out the rigging of a schooner
a mile off; I can count
the new cones on the spruce. It is so still
the pale bay wears a milky skin, the sky
no clouds, except for one long, carded horse's-tail.

The islands haven't shifted since last summer,
even if I like to pretend they have
—drifting, in a dreamy sort of way,
a little north, a little south or sidewise,
and that they're free within the blue frontiers of bay.

This month, our favorite one is full of flowers:
Buttercups, Red Clover, Purple Vetch,
Hawkweed still burning, Daisies pied, Eyebright,
the Fragrant Bedstraw's incandescent stars,
and more, returned, to paint the meadows with delight.

The Goldfinches are back, or others like them,
and the White-throated Sparrow's five-note song,
pleading and pleading, brings tears to the eyes.
Nature repeats herself, or almost does:
repeat, repeat, repeat; revise, revise, revise.

Years ago, you told me it was here
(in 1932?) you first "discovered *girls*"
and learned to sail, and learned to kiss.
You had "such fun," you said, that classic summer.
("Fun"—it always seemed to leave you at a loss . . .)

You left North Haven, anchored in its rock,
afloat in mystic blue . . . And now—you've left
for good. You can't derange, or re-arrange,
your poems again. (But the Sparrows can their song.)
The words won't change again. Sad friend, you cannot change.

ROBERT HAYDEN

Paul Laurence Dunbar

(for Herbert Martin)

We lay red roses on his grave,
speak sorrowfully of him
as if he were but newly dead

And so it seems to us
this raw spring day, though years
before we two were born he was
a young poet dead.

Poet of our youth—
his "cri du coeur" our own,
his verses "in a broken tongue"

beguiling as an elder
brother's antic lore.
Their sad blackface lilt and croon
survive him like

The happy look (subliminal
of victim, dying man)
a summer's tintypes hold.

The roses flutter in the wind;
we weight their stems
with stones, then drive away.

JOHN BERRYMAN

I have moved to Dublin . . .

from *The Dream Songs* (312)

I have moved to Dublin to have it out with you,
majestic Shade, You whom I read so well
so many years ago,
did I read your lesson right? did I see through
your phases to the real? your heaven, your hell
did I enquire properly into?

For years then I forgot you, I put you down,
ingratitude is the necessary curse
of making things new:
I brought my family to see me through,
I brought my homage & my soft remorse,
I brought a book or two

only, including in the end your last
strange poems made under the shadow of death
Your high figures float
again across my mind and all your past
fills my walled garden with your honey breath
wherein I move, a mote.

MAXINE KUMIN

How It Is

Shall I say how it is in your clothes?
A month after your death I wear your blue jacket.
The dog at the center of my life recognizes
you've come to visit, he's ecstatic.
In the left pocket, a hole.
In the right, a parking ticket
delivered up last August on Bay State Road.
In my heart, a scatter like milkweed,
a flinging from the pods of the soul.
My skin presses your old outline.
It is hot and dry inside.

I think of the last day of your life,
old friend, how I would unwind it, paste
it together in a different collage,
back from the death car idling in the garage,
back up the stairs, your praying hands unlaced,
reassembling the bits of bread and tuna fish
into a ceremony of sandwich,
running the home movie backward to a space
we could be easy in, a kitchen place
with vodka and ice, our words like living meat.

Dear friend, you have excited crowds
with your example. They swell
like wine bags, straining at your seams.
I will be years gathering up our words,
fishing out letters, snapshots, stains,
leaning my ribs against this durable cloth
to put on the dumb blue blazer of your death.

W. S. MERWIN

Lament for the Makers

I that all through my early days
I remember well was always
    the youngest of the company
    save for one sister after me

from the time when I was able
to walk under the dinner table
    and be punished for that promptly
    because its leaves could fall on me

father and mother overhead
who they talked with and what they said
    were mostly clouds that knew already
    directions far too old for me

at school I skipped a grade so that
whatever I did after that
    each year everyone would be
    older and hold it up to me

at college many of my friends
were returning veterans
    equipped with an authority
    I admired and they treated me

as the kid some years below them
so I married half to show them
    and listened with new vanity
    when I heard it said of me

how young I was and what a shock
I was the youngest on the block
    I thought I had it coming to me
    and I believe it mattered to me

and seemed my own and there to stay
for a while then came the day
    I was in another country
    other older friends around me

my youth by then taken for granted
and found that it had been supplanted
    the notes in some anthology
    listed persons born after me

how long had that been going on
how could I be not quite so young
    and not notice and nobody
    even bother to inform me

though my fond hopes were taking longer
than I had hoped when I was younger
    a phrase that came more frequently
    to suggest itself to me

but the secret was still there
safe in the unprotected air
    that breath that in its own words only
    sang when I was a child to me

and caught me helpless to convey it
with nothing but the words to say it
    though it was those words completely
    and they rang it was clear to me

with a changeless overtone
I have listened for since then
    hearing that note endlessly
    vary every time beyond me

trying to find where it comes from
and to what words it may come
    and forever after be
    present for the thought kept at me

that my mother and every day
of our lives would slip away
    like the summer and suddenly
    all would have been taken from me

but that presence I had known
sometimes in words would not be gone
    and if it spoke even once for me
    it would stay there and be me

however few might choose those words
for listening to afterwards
    there I would be awake to see
    a world that looked unchanged to me

I suppose that was what I thought
young as I was then and that note
    sang from the words of somebody
    in my twenties I looked around me

to all the poets who were then
living and whose lines had been
    sustenance and company
    and a light for years to me

I found the portraits of their faces
first in the rows of oval spaces
    in Oscar Williams' *Treasury*
    so they were settled long before me

and they would always be the same
in that distance of their fame
    affixed in immortality
    during their lifetimes while around me

all was woods seen from a train
no sooner glimpsed than gone again
    but those immortals constantly
    in some measure reassured me

then first there was Dylan Thomas
from the White Horse taken from us
    to the brick wall I woke to see
    for years across the street from me

then word of the death of Stevens
brought a new knowledge of silence
    the nothing not there finally
    the sparrow saying Bethou me

how long his long auroras had
played on the darkness overhead
    since I looked up from my Shelley
    and Arrowsmith first showed him to me

and not long from his death until
Edwin Muir had fallen still
    that fine bell of the latter day
    not well heard yet it seems to me

Sylvia Plath then took her own
direction into the unknown
    from her last stars and poetry
    in the house a few blocks from me

Williams a little afterwards
was carried off by the black rapids
    that flowed through Paterson as he
    said and their rushing sound is in me

that was the time that gathered Frost
into the dark where he was lost
    to us but from too far to see
    his voice keeps coming back to me

then the sudden news that Ted
Roethke had been found floating dead
    in someone's pool at night but he
    still rises from his lines for me

MacNeice watched the cold light harden
when that day had left the garden
    stepped into the dark ground to see
    where it went but never told me

and on the rimless wheel in turn
Eliot spun and Jarrell was borne
    off by a car who had loved to see
    the racetrack then there came to me

one day the knocking at the garden
door and the news that Berryman
    from the bridge had leapt who twenty
    years before had quoted to me

the passage where *a jest* wrote Crane
falls from the speechless caravan
    with a wave to bones and Henry
    and to all that he had told me

I dreamed that Auden sat up in bed
but I could not catch what he said
    by that time he was already
    dead someone next morning told me

and Marianne Moore entered the ark
Pound would say no more from the dark
    who once had helped to set me free
    I thought of the prose around me

and David Jones would rest until
the turn of time under the hill
    but from the sleep of Arthur he
    wakes an echo that follows me

Lowell thought the shadow skyline
coming toward him was Manhattan
    but it blacked out in the taxi
    once he read his *Notebook* to me

at the number he had uttered
to the driver a last word
    then that watchful and most lonely
    wanderer whose words went with me

everywhere Elizabeth
Bishop lay alone in death
    they were leaving the party early
    our elders it came home to me

but the needle moved among us
taking always by surprise
    flicking by too fast to see
    to touch a friend born after me

and James Wright by his darkened river
heard the night heron pass over
    took his candle down the frosty
    road and disappeared before me

Howard Moss had felt the gnawing
at his name and found that nothing
    made it better he was funny
    even so about it to me

Graves in his nineties lost the score
forgot that he had died before
    found his way back innocently
    who once had been a guide to me

Nemerov sadder than his verse
said a new year could not be worse
    then the black flukes of agony
    went down leaving the words with me

Stafford watched his hand catch the light
seeing that it was time to write
    a memento of their story
    signed and is a plain before me

now Jimmy Merrill's voice is heard
like an aria afterward
    and we know he will never be
    old after all who spoke to me

on the cold street that last evening
of his heart that leapt at finding
    some yet unknown poetry
    then waved through the window to me

in that city we were born in
one by one they have all gone
    out of the time and language we
    had in common which have brought me

to this season after them
the best words did not keep them from
    leaving themselves finally
    as this day is going from me

and the clear note they were hearing
never promised anything
    but the true sound of brevity
    that will go on after me

ANNE SEXTON

Sylvia's Death

for Sylvia Plath

O Sylvia, Sylvia,
with a dead box of stones and spoons,

with two children, two meteors
wandering loose in the tiny playroom,

with your mouth into the sheet,
into the roofbeam, into the dumb prayer,

(Sylvia, Sylvia,
where did you go
after you wrote me
from Devonshire
about raising potatoes
and keeping bees?)

what did you stand by,
just how did you lie down into?

Thief! —
how did you crawl into,

crawl down alone
into the death I wanted so badly and for so long,

the death we said we both outgrew,
the one we wore on our skinny breasts,

the one we talked of so often each time
we downed three extra dry martinis in Boston,

the death that talked of analysts and cures,
the death that talked like brides with plots,

the death we drank to,
the motives and then the quiet deed?

(In Boston
the dying
ride in cabs,
yes death again,
that ride home
with *our* boy.)

O Sylvia, I remember the sleepy drummer
who beat on our eyes with an old story,

how we wanted to let him come
like a sadist or a New York fairy

to do his job,
a necessity, a window in a wall or a crib,

and since that time he waited
under our heart, our cupboard,

and I see now that we store him up
year after year, old suicides

and I know at the news of your death,
a terrible taste for it, like salt.

(And me,
me too.
And now, Sylvia,
you again
with death again,

that ride home
with *our* boy.)

And I say only
with my arms stretched out into that stone place,

what is your death
but an old belonging,

a mole that fell out
of one of your poems?

(O friend,
while the moon's bad,
and the king's gone,
and the queen's at her wit's end
the bar fly ought to sing!)

O tiny mother,
you too!
O funny duchess!
O blonde thing!

WILLIAM DICKEY

The Death of John Berryman

Henry went over the edge of the bridge first; he always did.
Then Mr. Interlocutor and Mr. Bones, then the blackface minstrels
with their tambourines. You have to empty out
all of the contents before the person himself dies.

The beard went over the edge; and Stephen Crane,
and the never-completed scholarly work on Shakespeare,
and faculty wives, and a sheaf of recovery wards
white-taled in the blue shadow of the little hours.

He loosened his necktie and the recurrent dream
of walking out under water to the destined island.
His mother went over in pearls; his father went over.
His real father went over, whoever his father was.
He thought to go over with someone, hand in hand
with perhaps Mistress Bradstreet, but someone always preceded him.
The news of his death preceded him. It hit the water
with a fat splash and the target twanged.

When there was nothing to see with or hear with, the silent traffic
of bystanders wrapped in snow, his only body
let itself loose, turned and waved before it went over
to what it could never understand as being the human shore.

GARY SNYDER

For Lew Welch in a Snowfall

Snowfall in March:
I sit in the white glow reading a thesis
About you. Your poems, your life.

The author's my student,
He even quotes me.

Forty years since we joked in a kitchen in Portland
Twenty since you disappeared.

All those years and their moments—
Crackling bacon, slamming car doors,
Poems tried out on friends,
Will be one more archive,
One more shaky text.

But life continues in the kitchen
Where we still laugh and cook,
Watching snow.

JAYNE CORTEZ

For the Poets (Christopher Okigbo & Henry Dumas)

I need kai kai   ah
a glass of akpetesie   ah
from torn arm of Bessie Smith   ah

I need the smell of Nsukka   ah
the body sweat of a durbar   ah
five tap dancers   ah
and those fleshy blues kingdoms from deep south   ah
to belly-roll forward praise
for Christopher Okigbo   ah

I need a canefield of superstitious women   a
fumes and feathers from port of Lobito   a
skull of a mercenary   a
ashes from a Texas lynching   a
the midnight snakes of Damballah   a
liquid from the eyeballs of a leopard   a
sweet oil from the ears of an elder   a
to make a delta praise for the poets   a

On this day approaching me like a mystic
number   oh
in this time slot on death row   oh
in this flesh picking Sahelian zone   oh
in this dynamite dust and dragon blood and liver
cut   oh

I need cockroaches   ah
congo square   ah
a can of skokian   ah
from flaming mouth of a howling wolf   ah

I need the smell of Harlem   ah
spirits from the birthplace of Basuto   ah
mysteries from an Arkansas pyramid   ah
shark teeth   ah
buffalo   ah
guerrillas in the rainy season   ah
to boogie forward ju ju praise for Henry Dumas   ah

In this day of one hundred surging zanzi bars   oh
In this day of bongo clubs moon cafes and paradise
lounges   oh
In this day's pounded torso of burgundy mush   oh
In this steel cube   in this domino   in this dry
period   oh

I need tongues like coiling pythons   ah
spearheads gushing from gulf of Guinea   ah
the broken ankles of a B.J. Vorster   ah
to light up this red velvet jungle   ah
i need pink spots from the lips of trumpet
players   ah
the abdominal scars of seven head hunters   ah
a gunslit for electric watermelon seeds   ah
to flash a delta praise for the poets   ah

Because they'll try and shoot us
like they shot Henry Dumas   huh
because we massacre each other
and Christopher Okigbo is dead   uh-huh
because i can't make the best of it   uh-hun
because i'm not a bystander   uh-hun
because mugging is not my profession   uh-unh

I need one more piss-ass night to make a
hurricane   a
i need one more hate mouth racist

sucking the other end of another gas pipe to make
flames   a
i need one more good funky blood pact
to shake forward a delta praise for the poets   a

On this day of living dead Dumas
on this day of living dead Okigbo

I need kai kai   ah   i need durbars   ah   i need torn
arms   ah
i need canefields   ah   i need feathers   ah   i need
skulls   ah
i need ashes   ah   i need snakes   ah   i need
eyeballs   ah
i need cockroaches   ah   i need sharkteeth   ah   i
need buffalo   ah

i need spirits   ah   i need ankles   ah   i need
hurricanes   ah
i need gas pipes   ah   i need blood pacts   ah   i
need   ah
to make a delta praise for the poets   ah

MARILYN HACKER

Ballad of Ladies Lost and Found

for Julia Álvarez

Where are the women who, *entre deux guerres*,
came out on college-graduation trips,
came to New York on football scholarships,
came to town meeting in a decorous pair?
Where are the expatriate *salonnières*,
the gym teacher, the math-department head?
Do nieces follow where their odd aunts led?
The elephants die off in Cagnes-sur-Mer.
H. D., whose "nature was bisexual,"
and plain old Margaret Fuller died as well.

Where are the single-combat champions:
the Chevalier d'Eon with curled peruke,
Big Sweet who ran with Zora in the jook,
open-handed Winifred Ellerman,
Colette, who hedged her bets and always won?
Sojourner's sojourned where she need not pack
decades of whitegirl conscience on her back.
The spirit gave up Zora; she lay down
under a weed field miles from Eatonville,
and plain old Margaret Fuller died as well.

Where's Stevie, with her pleated schoolgirl dresses,
and Rosa, with her permit to wear pants?
Who snuffed Clara's *mestiza* flamboyance
and bled Frida onto her canvases?
Where are the Niggerati hostesses,
the kohl-eyed Ivory poets with severe
chignons, the rebels who grew out their hair,

the bulldaggers with marceled processes?
Conglomerates co-opted Sugar Hill,
and plain old Margaret Fuller died as well.

Anne Hutchinson, called witch, termagant, whore,
fell to the long knives, having tricked the noose.
Carolina María de Jesus
tale from the slag heaps of the landless poor
ended on a straw mat on a dirt floor.
In action thirteen years after fifteen
in prison, Eleanor of Aquitaine
accomplished half of Europe and fourscore
anniversaries for good or ill,
and plain old Margaret Fuller died as well.

Has Ida B. persuaded Susan B.
to pool resources for a joint campaign?
(Two Harriets act a pageant by Lorraine,
cheered by the butch drunk on the IRT
who used to watch me watch her watching me.)
We've notes by Angelina Grimké Weld
for choral settings drawn from the *Compiled
Poems* of Angelina Weld Grimké.
There's no such tense as Past Conditional,
and plain old Margaret Fuller died as well.

Who was Sappho's protégée, and when did
we lose Hrotsvitha, dramaturge and nun?
What did bibulous Suzanne Valadon
think about Artemisia, who tended
to make a life-size murderess look splendid?
Where's Aphra, fond of dalliance and the pun?
Where's Jane, who didn't indulge in either one?
Whoever knows how Ende, Pintrix, ended
is not teaching Art History at Yale,
and plain old Margaret Fuller died as well.

Is Beruliah upstairs behind the curtain
debating Juana Inés de la Cruz?
Where's savante Anabella, Augusta-Goose,
Fanny, Maude, Lidian, Freda and Caitlin,
"without whom this could never have been written"?
Louisa who wrote, scrimped, saved, sewed, and nursed,
Malinche, who's, like all translators, cursed,
Bessie, whose voice was hemp and steel and satin,
outside a segregated hospital,
and plain old Margaret Fuller died as well.

Where's Amy, who kept Ada in cigars
and love, requited, both country and courtly,
although quinquagenarian and portly?
Where's Emily? It's very still upstairs.
Where's Billie, whose strange fruit ripened in bars?
Where's the street-scavenging Little Sparrow?
Too poor, too mean, too weird, too wide, too narrow:
Marie Curie, examining her scars,
was not particularly beautiful;
and plain old Margaret Fuller died as well.

Who was the grandmother of Frankenstein?
The Vindicatrix of the Rights of Woman.
Madame de Sévigné said prayers to summon
the postman just as eloquent as mine,
though my Madame de Grignan's only nine.
But Mary Wollstonecraft had never known
that daughter, nor did Paula Modersohn.
The three-day infants blinked in the sunshine.
The mothers turned their faces to the wall;
and plain old Margaret Fuller died as well.

Tomorrow night the harvest moon will wane
that's floodlighting the silhouetted wood.
Make your own footnotes; it will do you good.

Emeritae have nothing to explain.
She wasn't very old, or really plain—
my age exactly, volumes incomplete.
"The life, the life, will it never be sweet?"
She wrote it once: I quote it once again
midlife at midnight when the moon is full
and I can almost hear the warning bell
offshore, sounding through starlight like a stain
on waves that heaved over what she began
and truncated a woman's chronicle,
and plain old Margaret Fuller died as well.

CHRISTOPHER GILBERT

And, Yes, Those Spiritual Matters

Elegy for Robert Hayden

Whisper it,
"Oh Hayden,
he can do energy."

The words breaking in flower,
the breath on things
wearing bright new clothes.

The drums, bells, gods
in poemstate, speaking—
or hushin' each other.

The goofy dust
he threw in our tea materialized into
a story the class choked on.

Whisper it as he saw it—
intensely, the material part of being
is style.

Summons the Gabriel
half of him, the silent
leftover talk in your head.

9.

"If I Should Die, Think Only This of Me":

Self-Elegies

The genre that the critic Jahan Ramazani has called the "self-elegy" — "a self-standing meditation on the author's mortality" — is an ancient one that has flourished throughout the centuries, as the poems included in this section dramatically reveal. Its consistent theme is either an affirmation of, or a response to, the medieval Latin line that William Dunbar used as a refrain in his "Lament for the Makers": *"Timor mortis conturbat me"* — "the fear of death confounds me." Yet as the poems here will also demonstrate, there are nearly as many variations on this theme as there are poets elaborating it, though a number of these variations have plainly been shaped by history and circumstance.

For instance, awaiting execution in the Tower of London, the Renaissance poet Chidiock Tichborne muses painfully on his early demise ("And now I die, and now I was but made"), while in a very different context the Restoration writer John Gay insouciantly composes an epitaph for himself that stresses a cynical view of life as merely "a jest." A century or so later, the Victorian writers Alfred, Lord Tennyson and Robert Browning are both more pious and more sanguine, as they staunchly declare their faith in a life after death. Affirms Tennyson, "I hope to see my Pilot face to face / When I have crossed the bar," and Browning promises his dead wife, Elizabeth Barrett, that "O thou soul of my soul! I shall clasp thee again, / And with God be the rest!"

In the same century, though, Emily Dickinson defines dying with nervous skepticism as the "most profound experiment / Appointed unto Men." And more than a hundred years later, at the end of the twentieth century, C. K. Williams summarizes the dread at the heart of the dreadful medieval *"Timor mortis."* Watching a video of a holdup that ended in murder and listening to the victim's cry of "God! God!" Williams prays that "I want not, ever, / to know this . . . this anguish, this agony for a self departing wishing only to stay, to endure."

CHIDIOCK TICHBORNE

Tichborne's Elegy

My prime of youth is but a frost of cares,
My feast of joy is but a dish of pain,
My crop of corn is but a field of tares,
And all my good is but vain hope of gain;
The day is past, and yet I saw no sun,
And now I live, and now my life is done.

My tale was heard and yet it was not told,
My fruit is fallen and yet my leaves are green,
My youth is spent and yet I am not old,
I saw the world and yet I was not seen;
My thread is cut and yet it is not spun,
And now I live, and now my life is done.

I sought my death and found it in my womb,
I looked for life and saw it was a shade,
I trod the earth and knew it was my tomb,
And now I die, and now I was but made;
My glass is full, and now my glass is run,
And now I live, and now my life is done.

WILLIAM SHAKESPEARE

No longer mourn for me when I am dead (Sonnet LXXI)

No longer mourn for me when I am dead
Than you shall hear the surly sullen bell
Give warning to the world that I am fled
From this vile world, with vilest worms to dwell:
Nay, if you read this line, remember not
The hand that writ it; for I love you so
That I in your sweet thoughts would be forgot
If thinking on me then should make you woe.
O, if, I say, you look upon this verse
When I perhaps compounded am with clay,
Do not so much as my poor name rehearse,
But let your love even with my life decay,
    Lest the wise world should look into your moan
    And mock you with me after I am gone.

THOMAS FLATMAN

Song

    Oh the sad Day,
  When friends shall shake their heads and say
    Of miserable me,
Hark how he groans, look how he pants for breath,
See how he struggles with the pangs of Death!
    When they shall say of these poor eyes,
  How Hollow, and how dim they be!
  Mark how his breast does swell and rise,
  Against his potent enemy!
When some old Friend shall step to my Bed-side,
Touch my chill face, and thence shall gently slide,
  And when his next companions say,
How does he do? what hopes? shall turn away,
  Answering only with a lift up hand,
    Who can his fate withstand?
  Then shall a gasp or two, do more
  Than e're my Rhetorick could before,
Perswade the peevish World to trouble me no more!

JOHN GAY

My Own Epitaph

Life is a jest; and all things show it.
I thought so once; but now I know it.

ALFRED, LORD TENNYSON

Crossing the Bar

Sunset and evening star,
   And one clear call for me!
And may there be no moaning of the bar,
   When I put out to sea,

But such a tide as moving seems asleep,
   Too full for sound and foam,
When that which drew from out the boundless deep
   Turns again home.

Twilight and evening bell,
   And after that the dark!
And may there be no sadness of farewell,
   When I embark;

For though from out our bourne of Time and Place
   The flood may bear me far,
I hope to see my Pilot face to face
   When I have crossed the bar.

ROBERT BROWNING

Prospice

Fear death?—to feel the fog in my throat,
    The mist in my face,
When the snows begin, and the blasts denote
    I am nearing the place,
The power of the night, the press of the storm,
    The post of the foe;
Where he stands, the Arch Fear in a visible form,
    Yet the strong man must go:
For the journey is done and the summit attained,
    And the barriers fall,
Though a battle's to fight ere the guerdon be gained,
    The reward of it all.
I was ever a fighter, so—one fight more,
    The best and the last!
I would hate that death bandaged my eyes, and forbore,
    And bade me creep past.
No! let me taste the whole of it, fare like my peers
    The heroes of old,
Bear the brunt, in a minute pay glad life's arrears
    Of pain, darkness, and cold.
For sudden the worst turns the best to the brave,
    The black minute's at end,
And the elements' rage, the fiend-voices that rave,
    Shall dwindle, shall blend,
Shall change, shall become first a peace out of pain,
    Then a light, then thy breast,
O thou soul of my soul! I shall clasp thee again,
    And with God be the rest!

EMILY DICKINSON

This Consciousness that is aware (#817)

This Consciousness that is aware
Of Neighbors and the Sun
Will be the one aware of Death
And that itself alone

Is traversing the interval
Experience between
And most profound experiment
Appointed unto Men—

How adequate unto itself
It's properties shall be
Itself unto itself and none
Shall make discovery.

Adventure most unto itself
The Soul condemned to be—
Attended by a single Hound
It's own identity.

CHRISTINA ROSSETTI

Remember

Remember me when I am gone away,
   Gone far away into the silent land;
   When you can no more hold me by the hand,
Nor I half turn to go yet turning stay.
Remember me when no more day by day
   You tell me of our future that you planned:
   Only remember me; you understand
It will be late to counsel then or pray.
Yet if you should forget me for a while
   And afterwards remember, do not grieve:
   For if the darkness and corruption leave
   A vestige of the thoughts that once I had,
Better by far you should forget and smile
   Than that you should remember and be sad.

J. M. SYNGE

To the Oaks of Glencree

My arms are round you, and I lean
Against you, while the lark
Sings over us, and golden lights and green
Shadows are on your bark.

There'll come a season when you'll stretch
Black boards to cover me;
Then in Mount Jerome I will lie, poor wretch,
With worms eternally.

PAUL LAURENCE DUNBAR

A Death Song

Lay me down beneaf de willers in de grass,
   Whah de branch'll go a-singin' as it pass.
    An' w'en I's a-layin' low,
    I kin hycah it as it go
Singin', "Sleep, my honey, tek yo' res' at las'."

Lay me nigh to whah hit meks a little pool,
An' de watah stan's so quiet lak an' cool,
   Whah de little birds in spring,
   Ust to come an' drink an' sing,
An' de chillen waded on dey way to school.

Let me settle w'en my shouldahs draps dey load
Nigh enough to hyeah de noises in de road;
   Fu' I t'ink de las' long res'
   Gwine to soothe my sperrit bes'
Ef I's layin' 'mong de t'ings I's allus knowed.

RUPERT BROOKE

The Soldier

If I should die, think only this of me:
    That there's some corner of a foreign field
That is for ever England. There shall be
    In that rich earth a richer dust concealed;
A dust whom England bore, shaped, made aware,
    Gave, once, her flowers to love, her ways to roam,
A body of England's, breathing English air,
    Washed by the rivers, blest by suns of home.

And think, this heart, all evil shed away,
    A pulse in the eternal mind, no less
        Gives somewhere back the thoughts by England given;
Her sights and sounds; dreams happy as her day;
    And laughter, learnt of friends; and gentleness,
        In hearts at peace, under an English heaven.

EDNA ST. VINCENT MILLAY

Burial

Mine is a body that should die at sea!
   And have for a grave, instead of a grave
Six feet deep and the length of me,
   All the water that is under the wave!

And terrible fishes to seize my flesh,
   Such as a living man might fear,
And eat me while I am firm and fresh, —
   Not wait till I've been dead for a year!

JOHN BETJEMAN

The Cottage Hospital

At the end of a long-walled garden
    in a red provincial town,
A brick path led to a mulberry
    scanty grass at its feet.
I lay under blackening branches
    where the mulberry leaves hung down
Sheltering ruby fruit globes
    from a Sunday-tea-time heat.
Apple and plum espaliers
    basked upon bricks of brown;
The air was swimming with insects,
    and children played in the street.

Out of this bright intentness
    into the mulberry shade
Musca domestica (housefly)
    swung from the August light
Slap into slithery rigging
    by the waiting spider made
Which spun the lithe elastic
    till the fly was shrouded tight.
Down came the hairy talons
    and horrible poison blade
And none of the garden noticed
    that fizzing, hopeless fight.

Say in what Cottage Hospital
    whose pale green walls resound
With the tap upon polished parquet
    of inflexible nurses' feet
Shall I myself be lying

when they range the screens around?
And say shall I groan in dying,
    as I twist the sweaty sheet?
Or gasp for breath uncrying,
    as I feel my senses drown'd
While the air is swimming with insects
    and children play in the street.

DAVID WRIGHT

A Funeral Oration

Composed at thirty, my funeral oration: Here lies
David John Murray Wright, 6´2˝, myopic blue eyes;
Hair grey (very distinguished looking, so I am told);
Shabbily dressed as a rule; susceptible to cold;
Acquainted with what are known as the normal vices;
Perpetually short of cash; useless in a crisis;
Preferring cats, hated dogs; drank (when he could) too much;
Was deaf as a tombstone; and extremely hard to touch.
Academic achievements: B.A., Oxon (2nd class);
Poetic: the publication of one volume of verse,
Which in his thirtieth year attained him no fame at all
Except among intractable poets, and a small
Lunatic fringe congregating in Soho pubs.
He could roll himself cigarettes from discarded stubs,
Assume the first position of Yoga; sail, row, swim;
And though deaf, in church appear to be joining a hymn.
Often arrested for being without a permit,
Starved on his talents as much as he dined on his wit,
Born in a dominion to which he hoped not to go back
Since predisposed to imagine white possibly black:
His life, like his times, was appalling; his conduct odd;
He hoped to write one good line; died believing in God.

JAMES WRIGHT

A Dream of Burial

Nothing was left of me
But my right foot
And my left shoulder.
They lay white as the skein of a spider floating
In a field of snow toward a dark building
Tilted and stained by wind.
Inside the dream, I dreamed on.

A parade of old women
Sang softly above me,
Faint mosquitoes near still water.

So I waited, in my corridor.
I listened for the sea
To call me.
I knew that, somewhere outside, the horse
Stood saddled, browsing in grass,
Waiting for me.

DAVID YOUNG

After My Death

1

It will all go backward. Leaves
that fell in October will float up
and gather in trees for greening.
The fire I built will pull
its smoke back in while the logs
blaze and grow whole. Lost hailstones
will freeze themselves back into beads,
bounce once and rise up in a storm,
and as flowers unwilt and then tighten to buds
and the sun goes back toward where it rose
I will step out through shrinking grass
at one for the first time
with my own breath, the wax
and wane of moon, dewsoak, tidewheel,
the kiss of puddle and star.

2

It will all go on. Rimefrost, mist;
at the cracked mirror the janitor
will comb his hair and hum, three boys
will build a raft, chalk dust will settle
in blackboard troughs, trucks bump
on the railroad crossing, soft talk in trees,
a girl practicing her fiddle: I know this,
I keep imagining it, or trying, and sometimes
when I try hard, it is a small stone fern
delicate, changeless, heavy in my hand.
And then it weighs nothing
and then it is green
and everything is breathing.

C. K. WILLIAMS

Fragment

This time the hold up man didn't know a video-sound camera hidden
    up in a corner
was recording what was before it or more likely he didn't care, opening
    up with his pistol,
not saying a word, on the clerk you see blurredly falling and you hear
    —I keep hearing—
crying, "God! God!" in that voice I was always afraid existed within us,
    the voice that knows
beyond illusion the irrevocability of death, beyond any dream of being
    not mortally injured—
"You're just going to sleep, someone will save you, you'll wake again,
    loved ones beside you . . ."
Nothing of that: even torn by the flaws in the tape it was a voice that
    knew it was dying,
knew it was being—horrible—slaughtered, all that it knew and aspired
    to instantly voided;
such hopeless, astonished pleading, such overwhelmed, untempered
    pity for the self dying;
no indignation, no passion for justice, only woe, woe, woe, as he felt
    himself falling,
even falling knowing already he was dead, and how much I pray to my-
    self I want not, ever,
to know this, how much I want to ask why I must, with such perfect,
    detailed precision,
know this, this anguish, this agony for a self departing wishing only to
    stay, to endure,
knowing all the while that, having known, I always will know this torn,
    singular voice
of a soul calling "God!" as it sinks back through the darkness it came
    from, cancelled, annulled.

GRACE NICHOLS

Tropical Death

The fat black woman want
a brilliant tropical death
not a cold sojourn
in some North Europe far/forlorn

The fat black woman want
some heat / hibiscus at her feet
blue sea dress
to wrap her neat

The fat black woman want
some bawl
no quiet jerk tear wiping
a polite hearse withdrawal

The fat black woman want
all her dead rights
first night
third night
nine night
all the sleepless droning
red-eyed wake nights

In the heart
of her mother's sweetbreast
In the shade
of the sun leaf's cool bless
In the bloom
of her people's bloodrest

the fat black woman want
a brilliant tropical death yes

10.

"Death & Co.":

Meditations on Mortality

Meditations on the phenomenon Sylvia Plath once ironically defined as "Death & Co."—mortality and the pain, fear, grief, it inexorably entails—are of course at the heart of every elegy. But time and its threats, death and its randomness, often elicit more generalized musings from poets, whether despondent or rebellious, weary or wondering.

Perhaps the most renowned of these ruminations is Thomas Gray's eighteenth-century "Elegy Written in a Country Churchyard," with its famous remark that "The paths of glory lead but to the grave" and its insistence that in any case "Full many a flower is born to blush unseen." But poems on the same theme by later writers, from Thomas Hardy and Ezra Pound to Edna St. Vincent Millay, are equally incisive and perhaps even more precise. Recording one family's moves from a "high new house" to a tomb, Hardy laments the passage of "the years, the years" and notes how ultimately "Down their carved names the rain-drop ploughs." Similarly, translating and revising a Chinese text he entitles "Poem by the Bridge at Ten-Shin," Pound shows that the classic question formulated by the great medieval French poet François Villon, "Ou sont les neiges d'antan?" ("Where are the snows of yesteryear?"), poses a universal problem: "to-day's men are not the men of the old days."

Finally, Millay's comment on the pain with which such human evanescence confronts her summarizes a feeling common to all the poets whose works are included in this section, indeed to all those whose writings appear in this anthology:

> Down, down, down into the darkness of the grave
> Gently they go, the beautiful, the tender, the kind;
> Quietly they go, the intelligent, the witty, the brave.
> I know. But I do not approve. And I am not resigned.

THOMAS NASHE

A Litany in Time of Plague

Adieu, farewell, earth's bliss;
This world uncertain is;
Fond are life's lustful joys;
Death proves them all but toys;
None from his darts can fly;
I am sick, I must die.
   Lord, have mercy on us!

Rich men, trust not in wealth,
Gold cannot buy you health;
Physic himself must fade.
All things to end are made,
The plague full swift goes by;
I am sick, I must die.
   Lord, have mercy on us!

Beauty is but a flower
Which wrinkles will devour;
Brightness falls from the air;
Queens have died young and fair;
Dust hath closèd Helen's eye.
I am sick, I must die.
   Lord, have mercy on us!

Strength stoops unto the grave,
Worms feed on Hector brave;
Swords may not fight with fate,
Earth still holds ope her gate.
"Come, come!" the bells do cry.
I am sick, I must die.
   Lord, have mercy on us.

Wit with his wantonness
Tasteth death's bitterness;
Hell's executioner
Hath no ears for to hear
What vain art can reply.
I am sick, I must die.
   Lord, have mercy on us.

Haste, therefore, each degree,
To welcome destiny;
Heaven is our heritage,
Earth but a player's stage;
Mount we unto the sky.
I am sick, I must die.
   Lord, have mercy on us.

THOMAS GRAY

Elegy Written in a Country Churchyard

The curfew tolls the knell of parting day,
   The lowing herd wind slowly o'er the lea,
The plowman homeward plods his weary way,
   And leaves the world to darkness and to me.

Now fades the glimmering landscape on the sight,
   And all the air a solemn stillness holds,
Save where the beetle wheels his droning flight,
   And drowsy tinklings lull the distant folds;

Save that from yonder ivy-mantled tower
   The moping owl does to the moon complain
Of such, as wandering near her secret bower,
   Molest her ancient solitary reign.

Beneath those rugged elms, that yew tree's shade,
   Where heaves the turf in many a moldering heap,
Each in his narrow cell forever laid,
   The rude forefathers of the hamlet sleep.

The breezy call of incense-breathing Morn,
   The swallow twittering from the straw-built shed,
The cock's shrill clarion, or the echoing horn,
   No more shall rouse them from their lowly bed.

For them no more the blazing hearth shall burn,
   Or busy housewife ply her evening care;
No children run to lisp their sire's return,
   Or climb his knees the envied kiss to share.

Oft did the harvest to their sickle yield,
    Their furrow oft the stubborn glebe has broke;
How jocund did they drive their team afield!
    How bowed the woods beneath their sturdy stroke!

Let not Ambition mock their useful toil,
    Their homely joys, and destiny obscure;
Nor Grandeur hear with a disdainful smile
    The short and simple annals of the poor.

The boast of heraldry, the pomp of power,
    And all that beauty, all that wealth e'er gave,
Awaits alike the inevitable hour.
    The paths of glory lead but to the grave.

Nor you, ye proud, impute to these the fault,
    If Memory o'er their tomb no trophies raise,
Where through the long-drawn aisle and fretted vault
    The pealing anthem swells the note of praise.

Can storied urn or animated bust
    Back to its mansion call the fleeting breath?
Can Honor's voice provoke the silent dust,
    Or Flattery soothe the dull cold ear of Death?

Perhaps in this neglected spot is laid
    Some heart once pregnant with celestial fire;
Hands that the rod of empire might have swayed,
    Or waked to ecstasy the living lyre.

But Knowledge to their eyes her ample page
    Rich with the spoils of time did ne'er unroll;
Chill Penury repressed their noble rage,
    And froze the genial current of the soul.

Full many a gem of purest ray serene,
    The dark unfathomed caves of ocean bear:
Full many a flower is born to blush unseen,
    And waste its sweetness on the desert air.

Some village Hampden, that with dauntless breast
    The little tyrant of his fields withstood;
Some mute inglorious Milton here may rest,
    Some Cromwell guiltless of his country's blood.

The applause of listening senates to command,
    The threats of pain and ruin to despise,
To scatter plenty o'er a smiling land,
    And read their history in a nation's eyes,

Their lot forbade: nor circumscribed alone
    Their growing virtues, but their crimes confined;
Forbade to wade through slaughter to a throne,
    And shut the gates of mercy on mankind,

The struggling pangs of conscious truth to hide,
    To quench the blushes of ingenuous shame,
Or heap the shrine of Luxury and Pride
    With incense kindled at the Muse's flame.

Far from the madding crowd's ignoble strife,
    Their sober wishes never learned to stray;
Along the cool sequestered vale of life
    They kept the noiseless tenor of their way.

Yet even these bones from insult to protect
    Some frail memorial still erected nigh,
With uncouth rhymes and shapeless sculpture decked,
    Implores the passing tribute of a sigh.

Their name, their years, spelt by the unlettered Muse,
    The place of fame and elegy supply:
And many a holy text around she strews,
    That teach the rustic moralist to die.

For who to dumb Forgetfulness a prey,
    This pleasing anxious being e'er resigned,
Left the warm precincts of the cheerful day,
    Nor cast one longing lingering look behind?

On some fond breast the parting soul relies,
    Some pious drops the closing eye requires;
Even from the tomb the voice of Nature cries,
    Even in our ashes live their wonted fires.

For thee, who mindful of the unhonored dead
    Dost in these lines their artless tale relate;
If chance, by lonely contemplation led,
    Some kindred spirit shall inquire thy fate,

Haply some hoary-headed swain may say,
    "Oft have we seen him at the peep of dawn
Brushing with hasty steps the dews away
    To meet the sun upon the upland lawn.

"There at the foot of yonder nodding beech
    That wreathes its old fantastic roots so high,
His listless length at noontide would he stretch,
    And pore upon the brook that babbles by.

"Hard by yon wood, now smiling as in scorn,
    Muttering his wayward fancies he would rove,
Now drooping, woeful wan, like one forlorn,
    Or crazed with care, or crossed in hopeless love.

"One morn I missed him on the customed hill,
    Along the heath and near his favorite tree;
Another came; nor yet beside the rill,
    Nor up the lawn, nor at the wood was he;

"The next with dirges due in sad array
    Slow through the churchway path we saw him borne.
Approach and read (for thou canst read) the lay,
    Graved on the stone beneath yon aged thorn."

THE EPITAPH

Here rests his head upon the lap of Earth
    A youth to Fortune and to Fame unknown.
Fair Science frowned not on his humble birth,
    And Melancholy marked him for her own.

Large was his bounty, and his soul sincere,
    Heaven did a recompense as largely send:
He gave to Misery all he had, a tear,
    He gained from Heaven ('twas all he wished) a friend.

No farther seek his merits to disclose,
    Or draw his frailties from their dread abode
(There they alike in trembling hope repose),
    The bosom of his Father and his God.

THOMAS HARDY

During Wind and Rain

They sing their dearest songs—
He, she, all of them—yea,
Treble and tenor and bass,
    And one to play;
With the candles mooning each face. . . .
    Ah, no; the years O!
How the sick leaves reel down in throngs!

They clear the creeping moss—
Elders and juniors—aye,
Making the pathways neat
    And the garden gay;
And they build a shady seat. . . .
    Ah, no; the years, the years;
See, the white storm-birds wing across!

They are blithely breakfasting all—
Men and maidens—yea,
Under the summer tree,
    With a glimpse of the bay,
While pet fowl come to the knee. . . .
    Ah, no; the years O!
And the rotten rose is ript from the wall.

They change to a high new house,
He, she, all of them—aye,
Clocks and carpets and chairs
    On the lawn all day,
And brightest things that are theirs. . . .
    Ah, no; the years, the years;
Down their carved names the rain-drop ploughs.

GERARD MANLEY HOPKINS

Spring and Fall

to a young child

Márgarét, áre you gríeving
Over Goldengrove unleaving?
Leáves, líke the things of man, you
With your fresh thoughts care for, can you?
Áh! ás the heart grows older
It will come to such sights colder
By and by, nor spare a sigh
Though worlds of wanwood leafmeal lie;
And yet you *will* weep and know why.
Now no matter, child, the name:
Sórrow's spríngs áre the same.
Nor mouth had, no nor mind, expressed
What heart heard of, ghost guessed:
It ís the blight man was born for,
It is Margaret you mourn for.

WALTER DE LA MARE

The Ghost

'Who knocks?' 'I, who was beautiful,
  Beyond all dreams to restore,
I, from the roots of the dark thorn am hither.
  And knock on the door.'

'Who speaks?' 'I—once was my speech
  Sweet as the bird's on the air,
When echo lurks by the waters to heed;
  'Tis I speak thee fair.'

'Dark is the hour!' 'Ay, and cold.'
  'Lone is my house.' 'Ah, but mine?'
'Sight, touch, lips, eyes yearned in vain.'
  'Long dead these to thine . . .'

Silence. Still faint on the porch
  Brake the flames of the stars.
In gloom groped a hope-wearied hand
  Over keys, bolts, and bars.

A face peered. All the grey night
  In chaos of vacancy shone;
Nought but vast sorrow was there—
  The sweet cheat gone.

CARL SANDBURG

Grass

Pile the bodies high at Austerlitz and Waterloo.
Shovel them under and let me work—
                I am the grass; I cover all.

And pile them high at Gettysburg
And pile them high at Ypres and Verdun.
Shovel them under and let me work.
Two years, ten years, and passengers ask the conductor:
                What place is this?
                Where are we now?

                I am the grass.
                Let me work.

EZRA POUND

Poem by the Bridge at Ten-Shin

March has come to the bridge head,
Peach boughs and apricot boughs hang over a thousand gates,
At morning there are flowers to cut the heart,
And evening drives them on the eastward-flowing waters.
Petals are on the gone waters and on the going,
      And on the back-swirling eddies,
But to-day's men are not the men of the old days,
Though they hang in the same way over the bridge-rail.
The sea's colour moves at the dawn
And the princes still stand in rows, about the throne,
And the moon falls over the portals of Sei-go-yo,
And clings to the walls and the gate-top.
With head gear glittering against the cloud and sun,
The lords go forth from the court, and into far borders.
They ride upon dragon-like horses,
Upon horses with head-trappings of yellow metal,
And the streets make way for their passage.
      Haughty their passing,
Haughty their steps as they go in to great banquets,
To high halls and curious food,
To the perfumed air and girls dancing,
To clear flutes and clear singing;
To the dance of the seventy couples;
To the mad chase through the gardens.
Night and day are given over to pleasure
And they think it will last a thousand autumns,
      Unwearying autumns.
For them the yellow dogs howl portents in vain,

And what are they compared to the lady Riokushu,
      That was cause of hate!
Who among them is a man like Han-rei
      Who departed alone with his mistress,
With her hair unbound, and he his own skiffsman!

EDNA ST. VINCENT MILLAY

Dirge Without Music

I am not resigned to the shutting away of loving hearts in the hard
    ground.
So it is, and so it will be, for so it has been, time out of mind:
Into the darkness they go, the wise and the lovely. Crowned
With lilies and with laurel they go; but I am not resigned.

Lovers and thinkers, into the earth with you.
Be one with the dull, the indiscriminate dust.
A fragment of what you felt, of what you knew,
A formula, a phrase remains, — but the best is lost.

The answers quick and keen, the honest look, the laughter, the love, —
They are gone. They are gone to feed the roses. Elegant and curled
Is the blossom. Fragrant is the blossom. I know. But I do not approve.
More precious was the light in your eyes than all the roses in the world.

Down, down, down into the darkness of the grave
Gently they go, the beautiful, the tender, the kind;
Quietly they go, the intelligent, the witty, the brave.
I know. But I do not approve. And I am not resigned.

STEVIE SMITH

Not Waving but Drowning

Nobody heard him, the dead man,
But still he lay moaning:
I was much further out than you thought
And not waving but drowning.

Poor chap, he always loved larking
And now he's dead
It must have been too cold for him his heart gave way,
They said.

Oh, no no no, it was too cold always
(Still the dead one lay moaning)
I was much too far out all my life
And not waving but drowning.

RICHARD EBERHART

The Groundhog

In June, amid the golden fields,
I saw a groundhog lying dead.
Dead lay he; my sense shook,
And mind outshot our naked frailty.
There lowly in the vigorous summer
His form began its senseless change,
And made my senses waver dim
Seeing nature ferocious in him.
Inspecting close his maggots' might
And seething cauldron of his being,
Half with loathing, half with a strange love,
I poked him with an angry stick.
The fever arose, became a flame
And Vigour circumscribed the skies,
Immense energy in the sun,
And through my frame a sunless trembling.
My stick had done nor good nor harm.
Then stood I silent in the day
Watching the object, as before;
And kept my reverence for knowledge
Trying for control, to be still,
To quell the passion of the blood;
Until I had bent down on my knees
Praying for joy in the sight of decay.
And so I left; and I returned
In Autumn strict of eye, to see
The sap gone out of the groundhog,
But the bony sodden hulk remained.
But the year had lost its meaning,
And in intellectual chains
I lost both love and loathing,

Mured up in the wall of wisdom.
Another summer took the fields again
Massive and burning, full of life,
But when I chanced upon the spot
There was only a little hair left,
And bones bleaching in the sunlight
Beautiful as architecture;
I watched them like a geometer,
And cut a walking stick from a birch.
It has been three years, now.
There is no sign of the groundhog.
I stood there in the whirling summer,
My hand capped a withered heart,
And thought of China and of Greece,
Of Alexander in his tent;
Of Montaigne in his tower,
Of Saint Theresa in her wild lament.

RICHARD WILBUR

The Pardon

My dog lay dead five days without a grave
In the thick of summer, hid in a clump of pine
And a jungle of grass and honeysuckle-vine.
I who had loved him while he kept alive

Went only close enough to where he was
To sniff the heavy honeysuckle-smell
Twined with another odor heavier still
And hear the flies' intolerable buzz.

Well, I was ten and very much afraid.
In my kind world the dead were out of range
And I could not forgive the sad or strange
In beast or man. My father took the spade

And buried him. Last night I saw the grass
Slowly divide (it was the same scene
But now it glowed a fierce and mortal green)
And saw the dog emerging. I confess

I felt afraid again, but still he came
In the carnal sun, clothed in a hymn of flies,
And death was breeding in his lively eyes.
I started in to cry and call his name,

Asking forgiveness of his tongueless head.
. . . I dreamt the past was never past redeeming:
But whether this was false or honest dreaming
I beg death's pardon now. And mourn the dead.

DENNIS O'DRISCOLL

Someone

someone is dressing up for death today, a change of skirt or tie
eating a final feast of buttered sliced pan, tea
scarcely having noticed the erection that was his last
shaving his face to marble for the icy laying out
spraying with deodorant her coarse armpit grass
someone today is leaving home on business
saluting, terminally, the neighbours who will join in the cortège
someone is trimming his nails for the last time, a precious moment
someone's thighs will not be streaked with elastic in the future
someone is putting out milkbottles for a day that will not come
someone's fresh breath is about to be taken clean away
someone is writing a cheque that will be marked 'drawer deceased'
someone is circling posthumous dates on a calendar
someone is listening to an irrelevant weather forecast
someone is making rash promises to friends
someone's coffin is being sanded, laminated, shined
who feels this morning quite as well as ever
someone if asked would find nothing remarkable in today's date
perfume and goodbyes her final will and testament
someone today is seeing the world for the last time
as innocently as he had seen it first

Contributors Notes

BETTY ADCOCK has authored four collections of poetry, including *Nettles* (1983) and *The Difficult Wheel* (1995). She lives in Raleigh, North Carolina.

ELLERY AKERS is the author of *Knocking on the Earth* (1989) and winner of numerous poetry awards. She lives in Marin County and teaches at the Bay Area Women Poets Workshop.

AGHA SHAHID ALI was born and raised in Kashmir. He has authored numerous volumes of poetry, his most recent being *A Country Without a Post Office*, as well as a critical work on T. S. Eliot. He is currently director of the writing program at the University of Massachusetts, Amherst.

FRANCISCO ARAGON is a native of San Francisco and longtime resident of Spain. He is the author of *Light, Yogurt, Strawberry Milk*. His work appears in the anthology *American Diaspora: Poetry of Exile*, and he is currently completing a bilingual collection of poems.

WENDY BARKER has published critical studies of Emily Dickinson and Ruth Stone, as well as three volumes of poetry, most recently *Way of Whiteness* (2000). She teaches at the University of Texas, San Antonio.

JUDI BENSON has authored a collection of poems, *Somewhere Else* (1990), and coedited several poetry anthologies, including *The Long Pale Corridor*, an anthology of elegies. She lives in London.

JOHN BERRYMAN, who earned widespread recognition and acclaim as a boldly original and innovative poet with his *Homage to Mistress Bradstreet* (1956), won a Pulitzer Prize for *77 Dream Songs* (1964). He took his own life in 1972.

JOHN BETJEMAN was made Poet Laureate of England in 1972. In addition to his many volumes of poetry, including *A Nip in The Air* (1972), Betjeman also authored numerous books on architecture. It is said that the IRA, thinking him a spy, once considered assassinating him, and then, on reading his poetry, decided otherwise.

JILL BIALOSKY's first book of poetry, *The End of Desire*, was published in 1997. She has received a number of awards for her poetry and is currently an editor at a major publishing house in New York City.

FRANK BIDART, who lives in Cambridge, Massachusetts, has authored numerous volumes of poetry, including *Desire* (1997) and *In the Western Night: Collected Poems 1965–90*. He teaches at Wellesley College and at Brandeis University, Massachusetts.

ELIZABETH BISHOP received many awards in her lifetime, including the Pulitzer Prize in 1955. She traveled extensively, and her sense of place influenced such collections as *North & South* (1946) and *Geography III* (1976).

RICHARD BLESSING published fiction, a children's book, and criticism, in addition to his poetry. His last collection was *Poems and Stories* (1983).

ROBERT BLY is a poet, translator, and critic who won the National Book Award in 1966 for *The Light Around the Body*. Since then he has authored and edited numerous books, his most recent poetry collection being *Eating the Honey of Words* (1999). He lives in Minnesota.

ANNE BRADSTREET, born in England in 1612, moved to Boston in 1630 and in 1650 published *The Tenth Muse Lately Sprung Up in America*, the first collection of verse to appear in the United States.

EMILY BRONTË, who died in 1848 at the early age of thirty, published her first book in 1846 with her sisters Charlotte and Anne, a collection of poems that sold two copies. Her great novel, *Wuthering Heights*, was pseudonymously published the next year under the name "Ellis Bell."

RUPERT BROOKE was a formalist poet most remembered for his "war sonnets," collected in his *Complete Poems*. He died during the first world war, at the age of twenty-eight, of blood poisoning from a neglected wound.

GWENDOLYN BROOKS was Poet Laureate of Illinois and received the Pulitzer Prize in 1950 for *Annie Allen*. An activist leader in the civil rights movement, she published over twenty volumes of poetry, a novel, and a memoir.

STERLING A. BROWN, who taught at Howard University for most of his life, published three volumes of verse, most notably *Southern Road* (1932) and *The Last*

Ride of Wild Bill (1975). Influenced by jazz and blues, he often used African American folklore to shape his work.

ELIZABETH BARRETT BROWNING was the foremost female poet of Victorian England. Still famed for her *Sonnets from the Portuguese*, she is increasingly well known for her verse novel, *Aurora Leigh*.

ROBERT BROWNING eloped with poet Elizabeth Barrett to Italy in 1846, where he wrote poetry that was, though not always well-received by the public, greatly admired by literary figures of the day.

RAFAEL CAMPO is a practicing physician at Harvard Medical School and the Beth Israel Deaconess Medical Center in Boston. He has won numerous poetry awards and published three volumes of poetry, including most recently *Diva* (1999).

LUCILLE CLIFTON's nine books of poetry include *The Terrible Stories* (1995), which was nominated for the National Book Award. She served as Poet Laureate for the State of Maryland and is currently Distinguished Professor of Humanities at St. Mary's College of Maryland.

WILLIAM COLLINS, known as a poet of "sensibility," published a number of influential odes, but suffered from poverty and illness for most of his life, and became insane before his death in 1759.

JANE COOPER lives in New York City and was the 1996–97 New York State Poet. She is the author of five books of poetry, most recently *Flashboat: Poems Collected and Reclaimed* (1999).

JAYNE CORTEZ is the author of seven books of poetry, including *Somewhere in Advance of Nowhere* (1996), and often incorporates performance or musical accompaniment into her work.

HART CRANE, an early twentieth-century American poet, is perhaps most renowned for his long poem *The Bridge* (1930). He died at thirty-three when he jumped overboard from a ship bringing him back from Mexico.

ADELAIDE CRAPSEY invented the *cinquain*, a poem of five short lines of unequal length. She did not live to see any of her poetry published, receiving notice of her first poem's acceptance for publication only a week before she died at age thirty-six.

COUNTEE CULLEN was a key poet of the Harlem Renaissance, though he eschewed the label of "black poet" and wrote in traditional forms, much influenced by Keats. His first volume, *Color* (1925), won the Harmon Foundation Literary Award.

E. E. CUMMINGS became famous for his radical and eccentric yet playful use of typography and punctuation. He published eleven volumes of poetry in his lifetime, including *Tulips and Chimneys* (1923), and a novel, *The Enormous Room* (1922).

PETER DAVISON, poetry editor for *The Atlantic*, has written numerous volumes of poetry and criticism, most recently *The Poems of Peter Davison 1957–1995* (1997). He lives in Boston.

WALTER DE LA MARE was known as a "Georgian" poet. His works include *The Listeners* (1912) and *Collected Poems* (1942).

JAMES DICKEY was a native Georgian and a novelist as well as a poet. Like his renowned novel *Deliverance* (1970), much of his poetry deals with the conflict of men against each other and against nature.

WILLIAM DICKEY was born and raised in the Pacific Northwest. He won numerous awards and wrote fifteen books of poetry, his last being *The Education of Desire* (1996). He died in San Francisco in 1994.

EMILY DICKINSON lived reclusively in Amherst, Massachusetts, and published just eight poems before her death, though nearly two thousand have been collected since, and she is now considered one of America's greatest poets.

JOHN DONNE is the best known of the metaphysical poets. Most of his poems remained unpublished until *Poems* (1635), published four years after his death.

MARK DOTY, the recipient of numerous awards and fellowships, has published five books of poems, including *Atlantis* (1995). He lives in Provincetown, Massachusetts, and Houston, Texas, where he teaches at the University of Houston.

RITA DOVE served at Poet Laureate of the United States from 1993 to 1995 and won the Pulitzer Prize for *Thomas and Beulah* (1986). She teaches at the University of Virginia.

CAROL ANNE DUFFY is a widely acclaimed British poet whose most recent collection is *World's Wife* (2000). She was born in Glasgow, Scotland.

PAUL LAURENCE DUNBAR, son of former slaves, worked as an elevator operator before being discovered by Frederick Douglass, under whose patronage he began his career as writer and lecturer. An important precursor to the artists of the Harlem Renaissance, he published eight books of prose and eleven volumes of poetry.

WILLIAM DUNBAR, of whom little is known but the work he left behind, was a Renaissance Scottish courtier, diplomat, and cleric as well as court poet.

DOUGLAS DUNN, professor of English at the University of St. Andrews in Scotland, is the author of several collections of poetry, including the award-winning *Elegies* (1985), written in memory of his wife who died of cancer at age thirty-seven.

STEPHEN DUNN is the author of ten collections of poetry, including *Loosestrife* (1996) and *Landscape at the End of the Century* (1991). He is currently a Trustee Fellow in the Arts and a Professor of Creative Writing at Richard Stockton College of New Jersey.

LADY CATHERINE DYER, of whom little is known, composed "My Dearest Dust" as an epitaph for a monument erected in 1641 in Bedfordshire, England, for her husband Sir William Dyer.

RICHARD EBERHART served as an aerial gunnery instructor in World War II and was Poet Laureate of the United States from 1959 to 1961. His *Collected Poems, 1930–1986* appeared in 1988.

ELAINE FEINSTEIN is a poet, novelist, and biographer who has written on the lives of Pushkin and Lawrence. Her volumes of poetry include *Daylight* (1997) and *Selected Poems* (1994).

JAMES FENTON has been a journalist, war correspondent, and translator as well as a poet. His books include *The Memory of War: Poems, 1968–1982* (1982) and *Out of Danger* (1994). He is Professor of Poetry at Oxford University.

ROY FISHER's books include *Poems, 1955–1980* (1980) and *The Dow Low Drop* (1996). He lives in Derbyshire, England.

THOMAS FLATMAN was a seventeenth-century miniature painter as well as a poet. He lived in London and published just one volume of verse.

ROBERT FROST is one of America's most celebrated poets. His deceptively simple verse, often couched in plain speech and traditional meters, caused many to dismiss him as provincial or conventional. He called poetry "a momentary stay against confusion" and won four Pulitzer Prizes.

TESS GALLAGHER is a poet and short story writer. Her most recent books include *Moon Crossing Bridge* (1992) and *My Black Horse* (2000). She lives in Port Angeles, Washington.

RICHARD GARCIA is the author of the poetry collection *The Flying Garcias* (1993) and of a bilingual children's book, *My Aunt Otilia's Spirits*. He is currently the poet in residence at Children's Hospital, Los Angeles.

JOHN GAY was an English poet and playwright best known for his political satire *The Beggar's Opera* (1728).

CHRISTOPHER GILBERT is the author of *Across the Mutual Landscape* (1984). He lives in Providence, Rhode Island.

SANDRA M. GILBERT's latest collection of poems is *Kissing the Bread: Selected Poems, 1969–1999* (2000). She teaches at the University of California, Davis, and is currently at work on a critical study of the elegy.

ALLEN GINSBERG was probably the most prominent figure to emerge from the Beat movement. His poetry drew extensively from mysticism, Zen Buddhism, and his experiences with hallucinogenic drugs. He published *Howl and Other Poems* in 1954.

LOUISE GLÜCK won the Pulitzer Prize for *The Wild Iris* (1992). Her more recent work includes *Meadowlands* (1996) and *Vita Nova* (1999). She is a native New Yorker.

THOMAS GRAY, a university professor, was a scholarly eighteenth-century recluse who published a number of melancholy odes but is best remembered for his "Elegy Written in a Country Churchyard."

THOM GUNN is a British-born but San Francisco–based poet who teaches at the University of California at Berkeley. He has published more than thirty collections of verse, including *The Man with Night Sweats* (1992) and *Frontiers of Gossip* (1998).

IVOR GURNEY was a British poet, much of whose verse came from his experiences at the front during World War I. At thirty-two, Gurney became schizophrenic and was committed to the City of London Mental Hospital, where he died fifteen years later.

MARILYN HACKER is the author of nine books of poetry, including *Presentation Piece* (1974), which won the National Book Award, and *Squares and Courtyards* (2000). She lives in New York and Paris.

DONALD HALL is the author of over a dozen volumes of verse, including *Winter Poems from Eagle Pond* (1999), as well as many books of prose. He lives in a farmhouse in New Hampshire that he shared with poet Jane Kenyon, in memory of whom he published *Without* (1998).

J. C. HALL was born in Middlesex, England, and has published a number of poetry collections, including *A House of Voices* (1973) and *Selected & New Poems, 1939–84* (1984).

MARY STEWART HAMMOND is a native Virginian and the author of *Out of Canaan* (1991). She lives in New York City.

THOMAS HARDY is best known for his novels, including *Jude the Obscure* (1895) and *Tess of the D'Urbervilles* (1891), but he also wrote much influential poetry, dedicating the last thirty years of his life to verse.

TONY HARRISON has written films and quite a few plays, many of which he has directed himself. His poetry volumes include *Permanently Bard* (1995) and *Selected Poems* (1999).

ROBERT HAYDEN grew up in the slums of Detroit and later studied with W. H. Auden. Though a formalist, he turned increasingly to forms of his own devising. His books include *Angle of Ascent* (1975) and *American Journal* (1979).

SEAMUS HEANEY, a Northern Irish poet, won the Nobel Prize for Literature in 1995. He recently published *Open Ground: Poems 1966–1996* and a new translation of *Beowulf* (2000).

WILLIAM HEYEN's poetry volumes include *Erika: Poems of the Holocaust* (1984) and *The Host: Selected Poetry, 1965–1990* (1994). He is currently professor of English and poet in residence at the State University of New York College at Brockport.

THOMAS HOOD was an English poet and humorist who, in addition to much light verse, wrote more serious works of social protest, including "The Song of the Shirt" (1843).

GERARD MANLEY HOPKINS was an ordained Jesuit priest in addition to being a poet. Although a Victorian, he remained unpublished until 1918, when his innovative techniques began to influence many modern poets.

A. E. HOUSMAN was an accomplished classicist whose first collection, *A Shropshire Lad* (1896), published at his own expense, immediately established his reputation as a poet.

LANGSTON HUGHES was a major figure in the Harlem Renaissance, and in addition to poetry, wrote fiction, drama, screenplays, essays, and autobiography. Among his many volumes of verse are *The Weary Blues* (1926), *Not Without Laughter* (1930), and *Montage of a Dream Deferred* (1951).

RANDALL JARRELL was a poet, novelist, and critic. He served in the air force in World War II, writing some of the best and most authentic poetry of the war from that experience. He died at fifty-one when he was struck by a car.

BEN JONSON started his career in the theater first as actor, then as playwright, and was imprisoned twice—not for killing a man in a duel (for which he was acquitted) but for two plays: one "lewd," the other offensive to the Scots. He was a great satirist and wrote poetry in a variety of forms.

SHIRLEY KAUFMAN lives in Jerusalem and has translated and written many books of poetry, including *Rivers of Salt* (1993) and *Roots in the Air* (1996).

X. J. KENNEDY, a critic and poet, has published *Selected Poems* (1985) and *Elympics* (1999), among other volumes. He lives in Lexington, Massachusetts.

RUDYARD KIPLING is best known for his poetry and fiction, including the *Jungle Books* (1894, 1895) and *Kim* (1901), about the British colonial experience in India in the late nineteenth century. He received the Nobel Prize for Literature in 1907.

CAROLYN KIZER won the Pulitzer Prize for Poetry for *Yin* (1985) and has authored six other volumes of verse, among them *Mermaids in the Basement* (1986) and *Harping On: Poems, 1985–1995* (1996).

YUSEF KOMUNYAKAA was raised in rural Louisiana and served as a war correspondent in the Vietnam War. His books include *Dien Cau Dau* (1984), *Neon Vernacular* (1993), which won the Pulitzer Prize, and *Thieves of Paradise* (2000). He teaches at Princeton University.

MAXINE KUMIN lives in New Hampshire. The author of eleven volumes of poetry, four novels, a collection of short stories, more than twenty children's books, and three books of essays, she received the Pulitzer Prize for *Up Country: Poems of New England* (1974).

PHILIP LARKIN was a highly influential twentieth-century English poet, though he published only four volumes during his lifetime, including *The North Ship* (1945) and *High Windows* (1974).

D. H. LAWRENCE, an innovative modern novelist and poet, was initially condemned for producing "indecent" literature. His novels include *Sons and Lovers* (1913) and *The Rainbow* (1915). Some of his best poems appeared in *Birds, Beasts, and Flowers* (1923).

LI-YOUNG LEE was born in Indonesia of Chinese parents and lived all over Asia before moving with his parents to Chicago, where he resides today. His books include *The City in Which I Love You* (1990) and *The Winged Seed* (1995).

DENISE LEVERTOV wrote more than twenty volumes of poetry and four books of prose. *This Great Unknowing: Last Poems* was published in 1999.

AUDRE LORDE authored numerous volumes of poetry, including *Cables to Rage* (1970), *Coal* (1976), and *Our Dead Behind Us* (1986), as well as four volumes of prose, among them *Zami: A New Spelling of My Name* (1982).

ROBERT LOWELL, one of the first of the "confessional poets," produced numerous volumes of poetry, including *Life Studies* (1959), *For the Union Dead* (1964), and *Day by Day* (1977), which was published just a month before his sudden death in a taxi.

HUGH MACDIARMID was a leading member of the Scottish Renaissance of the 1920s and wrote much of his earlier work, such as *Sangshaw* (1925), in Lallans, a form of Scottish dialect. He returned to modern English with *Scots Unbound* (1932).

HEATHER MCHUGH has most recently published *Hinge & Sign: Poems, 1968–1993* (1994) and has produced four additional volumes of verse, two translations, and a book on aesthetics.

CLAUDE MCKAY was a Jamaican-born poet, novelist, and essayist who moved to the United States in 1912, eventually settling in Harlem. His most important volumes include *Harlem Shadows* (1922) and a best-selling novel, *Home to Harlem* (1928).

JOHN MASEFIELD was England's Poet Laureate from 1930 to his death in 1967. He is best known for his sea poems, such as those collected in *Saltwater Ballads* (1902).

EDGAR LEE MASTERS gained fame with *Spoon River Anthology* (1915), verse epitaphs revealing the secret lives of people buried in a midwestern cemetery.

PAULA MEEHAN lives in Dublin, Ireland, where she has been the recipient of several awards. She is the author of five books of poetry, most recently *Pillow Talk* (1999).

HERMAN MELVILLE is the author of *Moby-Dick* (1851), considered by many to be the greatest American novel. He turned to poetry late, after his novels failed commercially and critically.

W. S. MERWIN is the author of more than fifteen books of poetry, including *The River Sound* (1999), and his many awards include the Pulitzer Prize in 1970 for *The Carrier of Ladders*. He lives in Hawaii.

CHARLOTTE MEW was initially a short story writer and only turned to poetry in her forties. Her most important verses appeared in *The Farmer's Bride* (1916). After sinking into obscurity, lonely and impoverished, she committed suicide by drinking a bottle of Lysol.

ALICE MEYNELL was a suffragist and a pacifist, whose first book of poems, *Preludes*, appeared in 1875. She went on to publish many books of poems and essays.

EDNA ST. VINCENT MILLAY, a glamorous figure throughout the 1920s, published plays and fiction in addition to twelve volumes of poetry. She received the Pulitzer Prize for *The Harp Weaver and Other Poems* (1923).

JOHN MILTON is best known for his *Paradise Lost* (1667), generally considered the greatest epic in English.

PAUL MONETTE was a poet, memoirist, and AIDS activist, who won the National Book Award in 1992 for *Becoming a Man: Half a Life Story*. He died of AIDS in 1995, after the disease had taken two lovers and spurred him to produce his best work.

MALENA MORLING was born in Sweden and studied in the United States. In addition to translations, she has published a book of poems, *Ocean Avenue* (1999).

CAROL MUSKE has written two novels and six books of poetry, most recently *An Octave Above Thunder* (1997). She teaches at the University of Southern California.

THOMAS NASHE was an English satirist and dramatist given to initiating extended literary feuds, one of which actually had to be ended by Ecclesiastical order. His work included *Pierce Penniless, His Supplication to the Devil* (1592).

MARILYN NELSON has published five books of poems and several books of verse for children. Her most recent collection is *The Fields of Praise* (1997). Since 1978 she has taught at the University of Connecticut, Storrs.

GRACE NICHOLS was born and educated in Guyana and came to Britain in 1977, where she now resides in Sussex. Her books include *The Fat Black Woman's Poems* (1988) and *Asana and the Animals* (1997).

DENNIS O'DRISCOLL is an Irish poet who has authored five books of poems, including *Hidden Extras* (1987) and *Weather Permitting* (1999).

FRANK O'HARA was an art critic and playwright, as well as a leading figure among the so-called New York poets, who were influenced in many ways by such contemporary painters as Jackson Pollock and Willem de Kooning. He published six collections in his lifetime, including *Lunch Poems* (1964).

DIANA O'HEHIR is the author of two novels and four books of poems, the most recent of which is *Spells For Not Dying Again* (1997). She is professor emerita at Mills College.

SHARON OLDS is the author of six books of poetry, including *The Dead and the Living* (1983) and *Blood, Tin, Straw* (1999). Named New York's Poet Laureate in 1998, she teaches poetry workshops at New York University.

GREGORY ORR has published numerous books of poems and essays, most recently *City of Salt* (1995). He teaches at the University of Virginia.

JACQUELINE OSHEROW has published four books of poems, including *Dead Men's Praise* (1999). She teaches at the University of Utah in Salt Lake City.

WILFRED OWEN was killed at the French front in 1918 at age twenty-five, by which time just four of his haunting poems of the war had seen publication.

LINDA PASTAN, Poet Laureate of Maryland from 1991 through 1994, has authored numerous volumes of poetry, including, most recently, *Carnival Evening: New & Selected Poems, 1960–1998* (1998).

MOLLY PEACOCK has published four books of poems, most recently *Original Love* (1995). Since 1979, she has directed the Wilmington Writing Workshops.

KATHERINE PHILIPS, a seventeenth-century British poet, formed the center of an intellectual circle called the Society of Friendship. Though she published few poems in her lifetime, she circulated many of them privately and became the best-known female poet of her age.

ROBERT PINSKY has published four books of poetry, including *The Figured Wheel: New and Collected Poems, 1966–1996* (1996), four books of criticism, and several translations, including *The Inferno of Dante* (1994). He teaches in the graduate writing program at Boston University, and in 1997 was named Poet Laureate of the United States.

SYLVIA PLATH produced her novel *The Bell Jar* in 1963, but remains most famous for the poems that appeared in *The Colossus* (1960) and, especially, in *Ariel* (1965), published posthumously after her suicide.

EZRA POUND is often considered the poet most responsible for defining and promoting the modernist aesthetic in poetry. For nearly fifty years, he focused on the encyclopedic epic poem he entitled *The Cantos*, published in sections throughout his life but never finished.

NAOMI REPLANSKI is the author of three volumes of poems, including *The Dangerous World: New and Selected Poems, 1934–1994*. She lives in New York City.

ADRIENNE RICH, activist and theorist as well as prize-winning poet and essayist, has long been an influential voice in the women's movement. Her most recent collections of verse are *Dark Fields of the Republic: Poems, 1991–1995* (1995) and *Midnight Salvage: Poems 1995–1998* (1999).

EDWIN ARLINGTON ROBINSON, though fame came late in his career, was one of the more acclaimed American poets of his time. His *Collected Poems* (1921) won the first Pulitzer Prize for Poetry, and he won another in 1925 for *The Man Who Died Twice*.

THEODORE ROETHKE's works included *The Waking*, which won the Pulitzer Prize in 1954, and *Words for the Wind* (1959). He taught for many years at the University of Washington, Seattle.

CHRISTINA ROSSETTI, a Victorian poet, is perhaps best known for her long poem *Goblin Market*, published in 1862.

CARL SANDBURG celebrated industrial and agricultural America in his free verse poems, especially in *Smoke and Steel* (1920).

SIEGFRIED SASSOON was posted at the Western Front in France during World War I, where he earned the nickname "Mad Jack" for his reckless bravery. That same spirit became manifest in his later poems, which criticized the war and the entire military complex.

ANNE SEXTON, one of the most acclaimed of the "confessional poets," won the Pulitzer Prize in 1966 for her third book, *Live or Die*. In 1974, after a series of breakdowns, she committed suicide.

WILLIAM SHAKESPEARE, a poet and dramatist, is considered by many to be the greatest writer the English language has produced.

PERCY BYSSHE SHELLEY was expelled at nineteen from Oxford for refusing to recant an atheistic pamphlet he'd published earlier that year. He left England and eventually moved to Italy, where he produced his best work. He drowned in a boating accident at age thirty.

TOM SLEIGH is the author of four books of poems, including *The Chain* (1996) and *The Dreamhouse* (1999). He has received numerous awards and teaches at Dartmouth College.

STEVIE SMITH authored several novels in addition to her more than ten collections of poetry, including her wry *Not Waving but Drowning* (1957).

W. D. SNODGRASS's influential *Heart's Needle* (1959) is credited (along with Lowell's *Life Studies*) with spawning the "confessional school" of poetry.

GARY SNYDER was born in San Francisco and spent most of his life on the West Coast, though his dozen or so years in Japan studying Zen Buddhism influenced his verse immensely. He has published sixteen books of poetry and prose and was awarded the Pulitzer Prize for *Turtle Island* (1975).

WILLIAM STAFFORD established his reputation and won the National Book Award in 1962 for *Traveling through the Dark*. He published *The Darkness Around Us Is Deep: Selected Poems* in 1993, the year of his death.

WALLACE STEVENS, one of the most important American poets of the twentieth century, was an insurance lawyer for most of his life. His major volumes include *Harmonium* (1923) and *Collected Poems* (1954).

ANNE STEVENSON has published a study of Elizabeth Bishop and a biography of Sylvia Plath in addition to her volumes of poetry, which include *Correspondences: A Family History in Letters* (1974).

JOHN STONE is a cardiologist as well as being the author of three books of poems, including *Where Water Begins* (1998), and a work of prose, *In the Country of Hearts: Journeys in the Art of Medicine* (1995).

RUTH STONE, who teaches at SUNY, Binghamton, has published seven volumes of poetry, among them *Second Hand Coat* (1987) and *Ordinary Words* (1999), which won the National Book Critics Circle Award.

JOSEPH STROUD is the author of three volumes of poems, including *Below Cold Mountain* (1998). He lives in Santa Cruz.

MAY SWENSON published eleven books of poems, several translations, and a book of criticism. She was an editor at New Directions, a visiting professor at a half dozen universities, and a chancellor of the Academy of American Poets from 1980 until her death in 1989.

ALGERNON CHARLES SWINBURNE was a nineteenth-century British writer who railed against Victorian social conventions in his plays, criticisms, novels, and poems, including *Poems and Ballads* (1866) and *Tristram of Lyoness* (1882).

J. M. SYNGE was the premier dramatist of the *fin de siècle* Irish Renaissance. He wrote his masterpiece, *The Playboy of the Western World*, in 1907.

JAMES TATE is the author of thirteen books of poetry, including *Worshipful Company of Fletchers* (1994), which won the National Book Award, and *Selected*

Poems (1991), which won the Pulitzer Prize. He teaches at the University of
Massachusetts, Amherst.

ALFRED, LORD TENNYSON was Poet Laureate of England from 1850 until his death
in 1892. His *Idylls of the King*, an epic retelling of the Arthurian legend, occu-
pied him for nearly fifty years, and his *In Memoriam* (1850), written to commem-
orate his friend Arthur Hallam, was a notable Victorian best-seller.

DYLAN THOMAS published his first book, the acclaimed *Eighteen Poems* (1934),
when he was just twenty. His work carried on a romantic tradition of intense lyri-
cism but was also influenced by the verse of his native Wales. He died from alco-
holism at the age of thirty-nine after a particularly long drinking bout during a
reading tour in the United States.

CHIDIOCK TICHBORNE was arrested and sentenced to be hanged for conspiracy
against the life of Queen Elizabeth I in 1586. It is said that he wrote his "Elegy,"
which he recited from the scaffold, on the eve of his execution.

HENRY VAUGHAN was a Welsh-born metaphysical poet who wrote two volumes of
secular verse, then turned to religious poetry.

ELLEN BRYANT VOIGT is the author of five volumes of poetry, including *Kyrie*
(1995). She lives with her family in Cabot, Vermont.

DEREK WALCOTT is a Caribbean-born poet, playwright, essayist, and painter who
won the Nobel Prize for Literature in 1992. His most recent publication is the
book-length poem *Tiepolo's Hands* (2000). He currently teaches at Boston Uni-
versity.

ALICE WALKER is a poet, essayist, and novelist, whose novel *The Color Purple* won
the Pulitzer Prize in 1983. Her most recent verse collection is *By the Light of My
Father's Smile* (1998).

WALT WHITMAN, often considered America's most influential poet, spent his life-
time writing and rewriting his masterpiece, *Leaves of Grass*, from the first edition
of 1855 to the seventh "Deathbed" edition, in 1891.

RICHARD WILBUR began writing in the army in World War II, an attempt to create a
measure of order amidst the chaos of war. He won the Pulitzer Prize in 1956 for
Things of This World and again in 1988 for his *Collected Poems*.

C. K. WILLIAMS teaches in the writing program at Princeton University and lives part time in Paris. His most recent collection is *Repair*, which won the Pulitzer Prize in 1999.

WILLIAM CARLOS WILLIAMS was a physician and modernist whose work ranges from compact imagistic lyrics to the book-length *Paterson* (1946–58) to several novels, an autobiography, and many short stories.

ALAN WILLIAMSON has authored numerous books of poetry and criticism, most recently *Res Publica* (1998). He lives in Berkeley and teaches at the University of California, Davis.

WILLIAM WORDSWORTH was one of England's greatest poets and with Samuel Taylor Coleridge outlined the romantic aesthetic in the preface to their jointly published *Lyrical Ballads* (1802).

DAVID WRIGHT was an English poet and the author of *To the Gods the Shades* (1976), *Metrical Observations* (1980), and *Poems and Versions* (1992), among others. He died in 1994.

JAMES WRIGHT produced eleven volumes of poetry, winning the Pulitzer Prize in 1972 for his *Collected Poems*. He also published a book of prose and seven volumes of translation.

JUDITH WRIGHT, one of Australia's foremost poets, has authored numerous collections, including *Human Pattern* (1999), as well as fiction, criticism, and children's books.

WILLIAM BUTLER YEATS, one of Ireland's greatest poets, devoted his life to theater, Irish Nationalist politics, and the study of mysticism. He was awarded the Nobel Prize in 1927. His major volumes include *The Tower* (1928) and *The Winding Stair* (1933).

DAVID YOUNG is the editor of the literary magazine *Field* and the author of many books of poems, including *The Planet on the Desk* (1990) and *At the White Window* (2000). He is also a critic and translator.

Permissions Acknowledgments

Wilfred Owen, "Anthem for Doomed Youth," and "Dulce Et Decorum Est" from *Collected Poems of Wilfred Owen*. Copyright © 1963 by Wilfred Owen. Reprinted by permission of New Directions Publishing Corp.

Linda Pastan, "Death's Blue-Eyed Girl" from *New and Selected Poems 1968–1998*. Copyright © 1998 by Linda Pastan. Reprinted by permission of the author and W. W. Norton & Company, Inc.

Molly Peacock, "The Fare" from *Original Love*. Copyright © 1995 by Molly Peacock. Reprinted by permission of the author and W. W. Norton & Company, Inc.

Robert Pinsky, "Impossible to Tell" from *The Figured Wheel: New and Collected Poems 1966–1996*. Copyright © 1996 by Robert Pinsky. Reprinted by permission of Farrar, Straus and Giroux, LLC.

Sylvia Plath, "Edge" from *Ariel*. Copyright © 1963 by Ted Hughes. Reprinted by permission of HarperCollins Publishers, Inc., and Faber and Faber.

Ezra Pound, "Poem by the Bridge at Ten-Shin," "Hugh Selwyn Mauberley IV," and "Hugh Selwyn Mauberley V" from *Personae*. Copyright © 1926 by Ezra Pound. Reprinted by permission of New Directions Publishing Corp.

Naomi Replansky, "The Six Million" from *The Dangerous World: New & Selected Poems 1934–1994* (Another Chicago Press). Copyright © 1994 by Naomi Replansky. Reprinted by permission of the author.

Adrienne Rich, "A Woman Mourned by Daughters" from *Collected Early Poems: 1950–1970*. Copyright © 1963, 1967, 1993 by Adrienne Rich. Reprinted by permission of the author and W. W. Norton & Company, Inc.

Theodore Roethke, "On the Road to Woodlawn," and "Elegy for Jane" from *Collected Poems*. Copyright © 1941, 1950 by Theodore Roethke. Reprinted by permission of Doubleday, a division of Random House, Inc.

Carl Sandburg, "Grass" from *Cornhuskers*, Copyright © 1918 by Holt, Rinehart and Winston and renewed 1946 by Carl Sandburg. Reprinted by permission of Harcourt, Inc.

Siegfried Sassoon, "The General" from *The War Poems* (Faber and Faber). Copyright © 1918 by Siegfried Sassoon. Reprinted by permission of the Estate of Siegfried Sassoon, through the Barbara Levy Agency.

Anne Sexton, "Somewhere in Africa," and "Sylvia's Death" from *Live or Die*. Copyright © 1996 by Anne Sexton. Reprinted by permission of Houghton Mifflin Company.

Tom Sleigh, "6. The Current" from "The Work" from *The Chain* (University of

Index